Total Communication:
Structure and Strategy

TOTAL COMMUNICATION

STRUCTURE AND STRATEGY

Lionel Evans

GALLAUDET COLLEGE PRESS
WASHINGTON, D.C.

Published by the Gallaudet College Press
Kendall Green, Washington, D.C. 20002

Library of Congress Catalog Card Number 81-85672

Gallaudet College is an equal opportunity employer/educational institution. Programs and services offered by Gallaudet College receive substantial financial support from the U.S. Department of Education.

ISBN 0-913580-75-9

CONTENTS

The growth of total communication as a major concept in the education of deaf children has produced some important questions about its nature, scope, and purpose. Is total communication a completely new philosophy, or is it a reformulation of previous ideas in the light of modern knowledge and resources? Why was this approach advocated, and with what supportive research evidence? Where, and in what way, is it being used? What are the linguistic properties of the constituent media, do they combine for enhanced efficiency, and how should they be ordered in a language development sequence? What is the teaching methodology for total communication, and what implications does it have in relation to other developmental needs and practical constraints?

This book briefly brings together information on these areas of inquiry. It reviews research findings and practical developments that have relevance to the concept of total communication and develops some theoretical ideas for language acquisition and growth.

Chapter 1 outlines some antecedents of total communication, then discusses educational attainments for deaf children and the professional attitude which gave rise to the philosophy of total communication, and traces the growth of its influence. Chapter 2 examines how widely, and in what way, it has been used in practice.

In order to understand the linguistic structure of total communication, it is necessary to know the strengths and limitations of its elemental parts. Chapter 3 looks at the problems of oral communication through speech and lipreading; Chapter 4 is concerned with fingerspelling; and Chapter 5 outlines different forms of signing—the salient linguistic properties and perceptual parameters of these media are explained. Chapter 6 deals with some of the perceptual processes and the communication effects in the simultaneous use of both oral and manual media.

For total communication philosophy to influence educational advance, the need for total communication theory and methodology is essential. Chapter 7 interprets the research findings and their relevance to the construction of a theoretical model of integrated oral and manual language development. Chapter 8 is concerned with the implementation of theory into practice. It sets out a methodological approach and examines some of the main implications for teachers, parents, and administrators.

The book offers an explanation of these problems for teachers—teachers of deaf children in particular, but also teachers of hearing children with language handicaps. As total communication occupies common ground between education, linguistics, speech science, audiology, and psychology, it should be of interest to professionals in these related disciplines. It assumes that the reader will come to the study of total communication with a basic knowledge of deafness and audiology and the problems deaf people have with written language. It also aims to provide an introduction to the more specialized research studies with a bearing on visual linguistic communication, some of which are included in the bibliography of suggestions for further reading. It is hoped that the organization of the chapters on a topic basis will make the book useful as a text for students.

From its origins in the United States, the concept of total communication has spread widely, and the book is written for an international audience. It must be pointed out, however, that for sheer simplicity, the linguistic examples refer, mainly, to the English language, or to systems for representing English—and there might well be some differences in other languages.

Washington, D.C.   Lionel Evans
June 1981

ACKNOWLEDGEMENTS

The writing of this book was possible by virtue of my holding the Powrie V. Doctor Chair of Deaf Studies at Gallaudet College for the academic year of 1980–81. I am especially grateful to Dr. Doin Hicks for his advice on all aspects of the project and his continuous support in carrying it out. I have benefited from countless discussions with members of the Gallaudet College community and enjoyed sustained encouragement from Dr. Clarence Williams.

I wish to record my gratitude for the willing and helpful cooperation of members of staff at schools where I made observations. I am pleased to acknowledge the criticism of the manuscript by Dr. Mervin Garretson of Gallaudet College, Professor Dennis Child of the University of Newcastle upon Tyne, England, and Professor Douglass Savage of Murdoch University, Perth, Australia, and I value the opinions of Mary Alexandra Coffey who read it from a graduate student's point of view.

I thank Grune and Stratton, Sydney, for permission to reproduce a number of figures from *Psychology and Communication in Deaf Children*, and the Royal National Institute for the Deaf, London, for permission to reproduce a chart from *Conversation with the Deaf*. I also acknowledge the contribution of William D. Lewis who prepared the original illustrations for the book.

I am happy to express my warm appreciation to Carol Bennetti, who was responsible for the preparation of the manuscript, and to Vivian Stevens for her help also at the word-processing stage.

Total Communication
Structure and Strategy

Total communication has emerged as a liberal approach to the use of both oral and manual means of communication for deaf people, but history records earlier attempts to teach deaf children through combined methods. Indeed, some of these practices may be seen as antecedents of the modern concept of total communication. An understanding of these past events might give a useful perspective for dealing with the present day problems, but within the context of the wider knowledge and modern resources now available. This opening chapter begins with a brief outline of some earlier practices, insofar as they might be viewed as forerunners of ideas that are now being brought together in the eclectic philosophy of total communication.

HISTORICAL PERSPECTIVE   It is generally considered that the systematic teaching of deaf people had its origin in sixteenth century Spain, when the deaf children of important families were placed in the care of Pedro Ponce de Leon. Because it was a legal requirement that these children should acquire speech to claim their inheritances, the prime emphasis was placed upon the teaching of speech. According to Farrar (1890), the order of instruction was "first teaching to write names of objects, then articulation, followed by the association of the written word with the spoken form" (p. 34). Another Spaniard, Juan Pablo Bonet, published the historically important book *Reduccion de las Letras, y Arte Para Ensenar a Hablar los Mudos* (1620), which included a one-handed manual alphabet. This book was eventually translated into English by Dixon in 1890, with the title *Simplification of the Letters of the Alphabet and Methods of Teaching Deaf Mutes to Speak*. Bonet believed that fingerspelling should be used by members of the family to the young deaf child. In his method, articulation of speech was based upon written and fingerspelled symbols. It is likely that Bonet's alphabet was an adaptation of existing systems, possibly one of the earlier Italian manual alphabets published in Rosselius's *Thesaurus* of 1579 (an illustration appears in Savage, Evans, and Savage, 1981).

The seventeenth-century English scholar John Bulwer produced the first books in English dealing with communication for deaf people. In *Chirologia*, or the *Naturall Language of the Hand* published in 1644, he used the term *chirologia* for communication on the hands "composed of the speaking motions, and discoursing gestures" (title page). To this he added *chronomia*, "or the Art of Manual Retoricke" comprising the "Naturall Expressions, Digested Art in the Hand, as the chiefest Instrument of Eloquence" (title page). He claimed that natural gestures, which he termed *chirograms*, were a form of universal language ex-

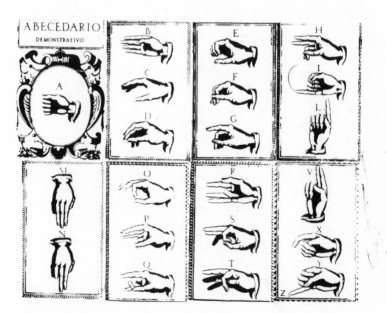

Figure 1. Spanish one-handed manual alphabet, published by Bonet in 1620

pression. He invented a system of communication on the fingers, which he called *arthrologie*, and in his *Deafe and Dumbe Man's Friend*, or *Philocophus*, published in 1648, he described "the Subtle Arte, which may inable one with an observant Eie, to Heare what any man speaks by the moving of his lips" (title page). This process he called *labiall augerie*. Bulwer thus advocated the use of processes which we would now think of as signing, fingerspelling, and lipreading.

A noteworthy theorist on the nature of language was George Dalgarno of Oxford. In his *Didascalocophus: or, the Deaf and Dumb Man's Tutor* of 1680, he described a primitive manual spelling system, in which letters were represented by pointing with one hand to parts of the other hand. He called his system, possibly the first to be devised especially with deaf people in mind, *dactylology*, a term which has continued to be used for fingerspelling up to the present time. He suggested that deaf children should be exposed to fingerspelling from an early age, in the hope that they might learn language in a way similar to that for hearing children. Dalgarno's system was not the form of fingerspelling which later became widely used in Britain. The earliest version of the British fingerspelling system dates from the pamphlet *Digiti Lingua* of 1698 which, with modifications, has evolved as the present day two-handed manual alphabet.

Another Oxford scholar of the time, John Wallis, also became interested in the problems of communication. His book *Grammatica Linguae Anglicanae* of 1653 (usually referred to as *De Loquella*) was written as a grammar of English as a foreign language. Wallis thought that this might be of value for deaf people, and in due course he became involved in teaching a deaf man. Some details of his method are known. From the use of spontaneous gesture, he proceeded to teach the written alphabet and gave separate attention to teaching speech articulation (Bender, 1970).

The Braidwood family claimed to use an exclusive oral

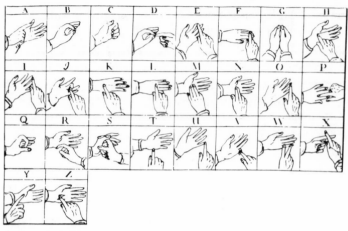

Figure 2. English two-handed manual alphabet, published in *Digiti Lingua* in 1698

method in the early British schools. However, after the death of the first Thomas Braidwood, his nephew, Joseph Watson of the school in the Old Kent Road, London, published his *Instruction of the Deaf and Dumb* (1809) in which he implied that the Braidwoods' success was based upon similar principles to the method used by Wallis—the use of natural gesture, written language, and speech.

The early teacher of the deaf in France, the Spaniard Rodriquez Pereire, was also secretive about his method, but an account written in 1764 by one of his most able students, Saboureaux de Fontenay (cited in Farrar, 1923) suggested that he also used signing, fingerspelling, and writing. Pereire adopted the manual alphabet used by Bonet but modified and augumented it in such a way that the hand formations represented not only the letters of written French but also the phonemes of spoken French. This phonetic system, for which Pereire adopted the term *dactylology*, may be viewed as an early forerunner of the nineteenth- and twentieth-century systems of phonetic fingerspelling and manual cueing of lipreading.

The serious study of sign language and signing systems

began with the work of Abbé Charles Michel de l'Epée at Paris. In his publications (1776; 1784) he described his teaching approach. In addition to speech and lipreading, he made early use of the manual alphabet, based upon Bonet's publication. He considered the language of signs to be the natural language for deaf people but set about to modify and expand it into his *signes méthodiques*—systematic signing of the French language. This was a forerunner of the modern systems for signing in the exact word order of spoken language. De l'Epée undertook the preparation of a dictionary of signs, which was eventually completed and published as Théorie des Signes by his successor as head of the Paris school, Abbé Roch Sicard (1818). When Sicard was, in turn, succeeded by Roch Bébian, there began a gradual reversion to the use of "natural" signs, used with fingerspelling to represent French syntax (Bébian, 1825, cited in Stokoe, 1960). The approach to teaching based upon the use of signing, fingerspelling, and written language, in addition to speech and lipreading, became known widely as the *French method* (in contrast to the *German method*, which was the name given to the pure oral teaching advocated in Germany by Samuel Heinicke).

When Henry Guyot founded a school for deaf children at Groningen in 1790, he based his teaching on the work of de l'Epée, but he was anxious to give greater prominence to speech and developed a combined oral and manual approach which became known as the *old Dutch*, or *mixed method*.

De l'Epée and Sicard also had an influence in England. Louis du Puget from Switzerland, who was familiar with the French method, was appointed head of the school at Birmingham and introduced signing and fingerspelling. When Charles Baker, who had trained under du Puget, opened the school at Doncaster in 1829, he developed a method which started with natural signing, was followed by fingerspelling, and led on to writing. William Neill, who had worked under Baker, was appointed head of the school at Newcastle upon Tyne, and he in turn introduced a com-

Figure 3. French one-handed manual alphabet, published in mid-nineteenth century

bined method. His successor, Andrew Wright, placed a greater emphasis upon speech. By 1891, he advocated a combined method using natural signs and the manual alphabet, leading to written language and the teaching of articulation and lipreading for those children who showed aptitude—surely an early forerunner of total communication!

The French method also influenced education of deaf people in the United States from its beginning. In 1815, the founders of the first public school for deaf children sent Thomas Hopkins Gallaudet to Europe. Gallaudet's intention was to observe the oral method in London and the French method in Paris. However, difficulties prevented him from studying the oral method of the Braidwoods, and in 1816, he travelled to Paris to observe with Sicard. Upon his return to the United States, accompanied by Laurent Clerc, he became head of the school opened in 1817 at Hartford, Connecticut, later known as the American School for the Deaf. He soon worked out the teaching method. The early use of manual signs was followed by teaching of more conventional type signs, then fingerspelling was introduced, followed by written language (American Asylum for the Deaf, Report for 1819, p. 6–8). The form of fingerspelling used was based upon the one-handed alphabet used in France at that time.

One of Gallaudet's two sons, Edward Miner Gallaudet, became the first president of the institution of higher education for deaf students at Washington, D.C., which was later named Gallaudet College in honor of the elder Gallaudet. The method of communication for instruction at that time included signing and fingerspelling with speech and lipreading. Edward Miner Gallaudet described this approach as the *combined system* (Gordon, 1892).

With the opening of further schools in other states, the use of manual communication in teaching remained dominant until the founding of the Clarke School at Northampton, Massachusetts, dedicated to pure oral teaching. Other oral schools followed. One significant attempt to modify the pure oral approach was made at the Rochester School for the Deaf in New York state. Zenos Westervelt proposed the use of fingerspelling, but only in conjunction with speech and in the correct grammatical word order of English (Westervelt, 1878). This became known as the *Rochester method* which has seen revivals from time to time.

By the later part of the nineteenth century, there were in the United States two broad educational philosophies, one advocating exclusive oral teaching and the other supporting the use of combined oral and manual media. In European countries, due largely to the influence of the International Congress at Milan in 1880, a more general adherence to

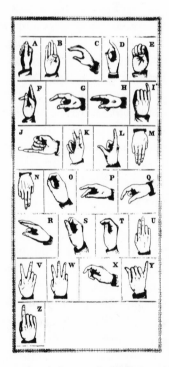

Figure 4. American one-handed manual alphabet, published in early nineteenth century

pure oralism prevailed. These were the traditions which persisted into the twentieth century.

A NEW APPROACH IN THE UNITED STATES   The middle part of the twentieth century saw new technical developments of great importance to the oral approach. The earlier invention of the telephone by Alexander Graham Bell and the discovery of the principles of electronic amplification of sound led eventually to the development of the audiometer for the measurement of auditory acuity and the hearing aid for amplification of speech. *Audiology,* the science of hearing and deafness, emerged as a new field of specialization.

One of the pioneers of the audiological era was Dr. Max Goldstein, who founded the Central Institute for the Deaf at St. Louis in 1914. He developed a scheme for training of residual hearing, named the *acoustic method,* which he distinguished from earlier oral and manual methods (Goldstein, 1933). The subsequent advances in audiological knowledge and technology have helped children with impaired hearing to use hearing aids to good effect. The modern concept of oralism emphasizes the early discovery of hearing loss, guidance to parents of young deaf children, and amplification of speech and training of residual hearing. To recognize the importance attached to the place of residual hearing for the reception of speech, the term *oral/aural method* has been applied for this approach.

Some use of combined methods, using both oral and manual media, persisted in the United States, mainly with older students. At the higher education level, Gallaudet College had a record of teaching through a combined method, using signing and fingerspelling in conjunction with speech and lipreading. The majority of the state schools for the deaf had a permissive attitude towards manual communication at the upper levels but were generally committed to oral teaching at the primary level. Most private schools and special classes in public schools maintained a pure oral outlook (Garretson, 1976b). By the mid-

1950s, it was the invariable practice in American schools to start young deaf children by the oral method (Elstad, 1955). It was claimed, in a study by Falberg in 1964, that sign language was not formally taught to students in American schools for the deaf, and where it was used in the classrooms, this was at the high school level (p. 35).

During the 1960s, the prevailing attitude towards teaching method became increasingly questioned by educators in the United States. Evidence of the results of the oral approach gave rise to dissatisfaction. Vernon (1971) surveyed studies by Schein and Bushnaq in 1962, Boatner in 1965, and McClure in 1966, which revealed that of the deaf student population, over 30 percent were illiterate, 60 percent were at a fifth-grade level or below, and only five percent reached tenth-grade level or better, and these were mostly hard of hearing or adventitiously deafened students. An important study of the actual attainments of deaf students on completion of their schooling provided further evidence. A survey of results of the National Achievements Tests standardization study carried out from the Office of Demographic Studies of Gallaudet College in 1974 (Trybus and Karchmer, 1977) found that in the twenty-year-old deaf population (who had passed through primary education in the 1960s) the average student had a reading ability below fifth-grade level; only 10 percent read at above eighth-grade level.

Although oral teaching prevailed in the early stage of formal education, some measure of the effects of the use of early manual communication was possible through observing deaf children of deaf parents. Comparisons were made between the linguistic and educational attainments of deaf children of deaf parents who had been brought up using manual communication and deaf children of hearing parents brought up with oral communication. Studies carried out with matched groups of children concluded that the early use of manual communication had a beneficial influence on various aspects of development, including general educational attainment (Stevenson, 1964), lipreading ability (Stuckless and Birch, 1966) and written language and social maturity (Meadow, 1968). Some experimental studies of work in schools also suggested that a combined method using fingerspelling with oral media promoted reading skill (Hester, 1963) and also written language and lipreading (Quigley, 1969).

Some caution is called for in the interpretation of matched studies. Deaf children of deaf parents are more likely to have hereditary-type deafness than deaf children of hearing parents. Consequently, the deaf children of hearing parents might have a higher incidence of brain injury, which could in turn adversely affect linguistic and educational development. Vernon and Koh (1970) carried out a study which took account of this possibility. They included as subjects only deaf children of hearing parents for whom there was positive evidence that they had deafness of hereditary type. Vernon and Koh still found the deaf children of deaf parents to have better educational attainment and were able to conclude that this was due to their early experience of manual communication.

An example of an experimental program aimed at developing the potential of a combined teaching approach with young deaf children was described by Brill and Fahey (1971). The California School for the Deaf at Riverside had previously used fingerspelling in conjunction with oral communication with children in grades one through twelve but considered that children under five years of age were usually not mature enough to learn fingerspelling of words. In 1969, it was decided to introduce signs with oral communication to preschool children, aged three to five years. Brill and Fahey observed the development of concepts, signs, and spoken and lipread words, and they concluded that the children made better progress than had been observed previously through pure oral teaching.

The children in the program had developed an understanding and communicating ability of over 350 concepts . . . . The speech and speechreading abilities are better in children who experience the combined system than with restriction to oral methods, and the social adjustment as demonstrated by their behavior is far better. As a result, the child's familial relationships, as well as his school ones, are appreciably smoother and more rewarding (p. 19).

Although the findings from research were widely regarded as evidence of the shortcomings of pure oral methods and the greater effectiveness of combined communication, acceptance was not universal. For instance, Nix (1975), in a review of research, questioned the interpretation of some of the studies. But actual events suggest that educators, in general, began to take a serious interest in the manual communication media in actual teaching methods.

Gradually there emerged a new attitude. Garretson (1976b) recorded that during the 1960s "a segment of the profession began to articulate the need to develop a philosophical framework that would recognize the value of manual modes as useful adjuncts to accepted aural/oral approaches" (p. 89). The theoretical interest in manual communication was heightened when such distinguished linguists as Lenneberg (1967, p. 320) and Chomsky (cited in Vernon, 1972) expressed critical views on pure oral communication for all severely deaf children.

Out of this growing concern there developed a more liberal outlook which advocated the use of oral and manual media in combination. This became known as *total communication*. Although the term had an earlier usage, as for instance in a work by Margaret Mead (1964), it has become associated with the liberal communication approach for deaf people. Garretson (1976b) records that the term total communication was used in 1968 by an educator, Dr. Roy Holcomb, to describe a flexible approach to communication in teaching deaf children at Santa Ana, California.

The term was quickly taken up, and in 1968 it was adopted by Dr. David Denton to describe the philosophy at the Maryland School for the Deaf. Denton (Note 1) described the approach there as comprising "the full spectrum of language modes, child-devised gesture, the language of signs, speech reading, fingerspelling, reading, and writing . . . the development of residual hearing for the enhancement of speech and speech reading skills."

The importance of fingerspelling and signing, to supplement the inadequacy of lipreading, has been emphasized. Vernon (1972) explained total communication as "a constructive coping with the reality of the limitations of lipreading. . . . the deaf child is taught and is given the opportunity to communicate through a system no more ambiguous to him than the spoken word" to the hearing child (p. 531).

The obligation of both hearing and deaf people to adjust their skills to meet the needs of the particular situation was stressed in a description of total communication as a concept that

involves the use of all means of communication with deaf people and by deaf people. It requires that a hearing person use his speech, signs, fingerspelling, and English syntax. It holds the deaf person to these same requirements. It also requires that every effort is made by the deaf person to use residual hearing (Merrill, Note 2).

The concept of a multimedia approach to communication gained further acceptance, so that in an international seminar held at London in 1975, total communication was said, by Brill (1976), to involve

the use of any and all modes of communication. This includes the use of a sign language system, fingerspelling, speech, speech reading, amplification, gestures, pantomime, drawing and writing . . . expressive modes can be used simultaneously such as speech, one of the forms of manual communication, and amplification. The individual . . . may receive through only one of the modes or by two or more modes simultaneously (p. 80).

The most significant departure from the pure oral approach was the recognition of signing, and especially sign language. There was, of course, not complete agreement about its use among educators of deaf children. Scouten (1973), although strongly advocating the use of fingerspelling with speech, questioned the concept of total communication on grounds that it undervalued the place for oral development and that the use of sign language might impair the development of English. Equally strong arguments were made in favor of sign language. Stokoe (Note 3) held the following view:

If total communication is to be what it claims to be, then it must include in its total more than just American English and all the many ways of coding it in visual symbols. Total Communication as a force in the education of the deaf must include the knowledge and use of sign (ASL).

It was pointed out by Stuckless (1976) that the term total communication "means different things to different people. To some, the one essential element is manual communication, to others, it is an assortment of techniques all of which have validity when used appropriately and selectively" (p. 143). Stuckless considered that "the legitimacy of the concept rests with the selectivity with which each potential technique subsumed under the concept is used" (p. 143). Garretson (1976b) recorded that there was broad agreement on three aspects of total communication: (a) it is "a philosophy rather than a method"; (b) it involves "a combining of aural/oral-manual media according to the communicative needs and the expressive-receptive threshold of the individual"; (c) it recognizes "moral right of the hearing impaired . . . to maximal input in order to attain optimal comprehension and total understanding in the communication situation" (p. 89).

To these observations Garretson added his perception.

Total communication is neither a method nor a prescribed system of instruction. It is a philosophical approach that encourages a climate of communication flexibility for the deaf person free of ambiguity, guess work and stress. . . .

Hierarchical distinctions among the various modes are avoided, each modality receives legitimate status as an acceptable instrument for human interchange (Garretson, 1976b, p. 90).

By 1976, interest in total communication had reached such a level as to warrant an official definition. The Conference of Executives of American Schools for the Deaf at the Forty-Eighth Meeting held at Rochester, New York, agreed upon a definition of total communication as

a philosophy incorporating the appropriate aural, manual, and oral modes of communication in order to ensure effective communication with and among hearing impaired persons (Garretson, 1976a, p. 300).

This hallmark of official recognition reinforced the widely understood concept of total communication as an eclectic attitude towards the selective use of appropriate media to suit the needs of the situation. Subsequent developments in educational practice emphasized this interpretation of total communication as a philosophical attitude towards the acceptance of oral and manual media, rather than a methodological prescription as to how they should be used.

This outlook was exemplified in the description developed for the Pre-College Programs at Gallaudet College, which held that

total communication is not a method, but rather a philosophy of approaching any given communication situation. . . . It is a recognition that not all modes of communication are effective for individuals in all situations . . . a commitment to a selection of those modes or combination of modes which will be most effective with individual children (Cokely, 1979, p. 9–10).

PARALLEL CHANGES IN BRITAIN   The trend in the United States was paralleled by developments in Britain, where concern for the level of educational attainment of hearing-impaired children led to similar changes in attitude and practice. During the 1950s, most of the formative influences on education of the deaf had been centered on a pure oral philosophy. Teachers were trained to use oral methods only; the communication research was concerned mainly with use of residual hearing, lipreading, and speech intelligibility; and the early guidance to parents emphasized the role of speech and lipreading. It is not surprising that, against this background of influence, the majority of British schools for the deaf aspired, at least officially, to use pure oral methods of teaching. The opening of many partially hearing units meant that by the mid-1960s the majority of children receiving full-time special educational treatment because of their impaired hearing were placed in ordinary schools. It was expected that when properly assessed, partially hearing children should be capable of making satisfactory progress in speech and language by oral teaching. With the continuing trend towards integration of hearing-impaired children in ordinary schools, the special schools became preoccupied with the needs of the more severely handicapped, and this brought into question the suitability of pure oral teaching for all deaf children.

In 1964, an important committee of inquiry was set up by the British Department of Education and Science under the chairmanship of a distinguished educator, Professor Michael Lewis, to consider the possible place of fingerspelling and signing in the education of deaf children. The report of the committee (Department of Education and Science, 1968) strongly endorsed a place for oral communication and urged improvements in the conditions for oral teaching. But it also recommended that research should be carried out to determine whether "the introduction of manual media of communication would lead to improvement in the education of deaf children" and to evaluate the "effects of combining oral and manual media" (p. 106). The publication of this report, popularly known as the "Lewis Report," opened the way for scientific study of communication in British schools in the 1970s, including evaluation of the results of oral teaching and the introduction of combined teaching methods.

In a study of communication methods, Rodda, Godsave, and Stevens (1974) commented on evidence suggesting that only a minority of deaf children educated by oral means attained intelligible speech and good lipreading ability. "How many children," they asked, "in how many places taught by how many teachers under differing oral regimes have to fail to make a viable educational progress before it is admitted that the oral technique is not so much a soundly based methodology but more a way of life?" They emphasized that, of course, some children benefit by oral education, and that all deaf children should be taught speech and lipreading, but questioned whether the small minority who achieve good speech and lipreading "represent a defensible position to warrant the formal exclusion of the other communication systems from the schools accepting the prelingually, profoundly deaf child" (p. 735).

In 1976, the Royal National Institute for the Deaf published the proceedings of an important international seminar on methods of communication currently used in the education of deaf children. Twenty participants from Great Britain, Ireland, Holland, the United States, and Canada presented papers. Of those experienced in education, psychology, psychiatry, or social work, some advocated the continuation of a predominately pure oral approach (Braybrook; Lowell; Reeves; Watson), but others proposed, or discussed evidence for, the use of combined oral and manual media for some deaf children (Brill; Craig; Davis; Denmark; Evans; Freeman; Meadow; Montgomery; Reed; Stuckless; Verney; Vernon). In a summary of these papers, Conrad (1976) commented on "the difficulty of assessing exactly what oralism has been able to achieve." He pointed out that, in contrast to "a very substantial body of research (into the use of combined media, there is) a curious, dramatic, and ... unfortunate imbalance in documentation (with lack of) a single published account which sets out the outcome, the achievements, and the shortcomings of good oral education" (p. 148).

It was Conrad himself who later provided sound evidence of the results of the predominately oral education in British schools. Working from the University of Oxford, with his colleagues Kyle, Morris, McKenzie, and Weiskrantz, Conrad (1979) carried out a comprehensive study of the actual attainments of virtually all prelingually deaf children completing their formal education in England and Wales during the period 1974 to 1976, a total of 468 children, of whom 359 were in special schools and 128 in partially hearing units. He provided a quantitive account of their attainments in communication and spoken and written language, their capacity for thinking, and their ability to internalize language and to use linguistic symbols. Conrad found a lack of satisfactory attainment in language development. Apart from general progress in language, as measured by reading and writing, the theoretical justification for an exclusively oral education must surely rest upon its special capacity to promote oral reception, oral internalization, and oral expression of language. Conrad's findings revealed that these specific criteria of oral success were not widely attained. He found unsatisfactory levels of lipreading, internalized speech, and spoken language.

The Lewis Report (Department of Education and Science, 1968) recommendations for research into the effects of combining oral and manual media were implemented, in 1973, in a developmental study of manual media in teaching methodology carried out jointly by the Northern Counties School for the Deaf and the University of Newcastle upon Tyne, with the official support of the Department of Education and Science. This involved the introduction of one-handed fingerspelling and signing, in conjunction with oral media in a combined method. It was confirmed that a new form of manual communication could be quickly learned by deaf children, and that combined media had a beneficial effect on reception and understanding of English language (Savage et al., 1981).

By the late 1970s, a number of British schools for the deaf had introduced combined methods of teaching or formally adopted the term total communication for their teaching approach. These include some of the older schools with past experience of manual methods, such as the Royal School for Deaf Children at Margate, the Royal West of England School for the Deaf at Exeter, and the Yorkshire Residential School for the Deaf at Doncaster, as well as some more recently opened schools, such as Heathlands School for the Deaf at St. Alban's, and Beverley School for the Deaf at Cleveland. In the south of England, the widening interest led to the setting up of a working party to develop practical guidelines for the most effective ways of combining lipreading, speech, residual hearing, signing, and fingerspelling into teaching method (Robson, Note 4). In Scotland, there has been research into the effectiveness of signing and fingerspelling (Montgomery, 1966, 1968; Montgomery and Lines, Note 5), and the term total communication has been widely applied for the combined teaching methods in Scottish schools. The support for total communication from professionals in fields allied to education included strong advocacy for the use of sign language. Verney (1976), a social worker, believed that "the manual component of total communication should be a standardized and systematized version of the sign language already in use by deaf adults" (p. 71). Denmark (1976), a psychiatrist, also maintained that total communication should include "the sign language as used by deaf people in this country" (p. 77).

THE WORLDWIDE TREND   The influence of total communication quickly spread beyond North America and developed into a worldwide trend. There is a close interaction between the United States and Canada in the field of education of deaf children. The concept of total communication quickly gained ground in Canada, where one of the strongest supporters has been Dr. Roger Freeman, a psychiatrist at the University of British Columbia.

As happened in other European countries, the Milan International Congress of 1880 had a strong influence on · teaching methods in Sweden, where sign language had earlier been used. For many years, deaf people had sought the reintroduction of sign language into teaching in the schools, but to little avail. The advances in audiology of the 1950s reinforced hopes for good attainment by pure oral teaching, but the "great expectations of the 50s were not realized. . . . Towards the middle of the 60s there was, in consequence, a growing interest in alternative methods of work and communication, and with it came a more open-minded attitude towards sign language" (Bergman, 1979, p. 9). This change of outlook led to some significant developments. Sign language was included as a subject in the official national curriculum of special schools. The Swedish National Association of the Deaf stongly advocated the acceptance of signing by parents for use at all stages of education and voiced a demand for the introduction of total communication into schools.

In Denmark, there has been a significant acceptance of total communication. By 1980, the majority of children with slight hearing loss were integrated into ordinary schools with varying levels of support. Partially hearing children were placed in special education units in ordinary schools. The majority of deaf, but also some partially hearing, children attended the four residential schools for the deaf. There was also a national residential college for continuing education beyond the compulsory school age of sixteen years. Most of the special education units, all of the schools for the deaf, and also the college of further education had adopted total communication. In Denmark, total communication includes the use of Danish Sign Language, Signed Danish, and the Mouth-Hand System for supplementing lipreading (Hansen, 1980).

The size of the country and the organization of the services for hearing-impaired children are conducive to a unified approach, but the Center for Total Communication has had an especially stimulating influence. Again, there is a strong emphasis upon the concept of total communication as an attitude towards the use of communication media rather than a way of teaching. The Center holds that

total communication is a communication philosophy—not a communication method and not at all a teaching method. ... Total communication is an approach to create a successful and equal communication between human beings with different language perception and/or production. ... To use total communication amounts to a willingness to use all available means in order to understand and be understood (Hansen, 1980, p. 22).

Denmark is renowned for its progressive audiological services and advanced hearing aid technology. The Audiologopedic Research Group at the University of Copenhagen supports and studies total communication, a fact which strengthens the view of total communication as a multimedia approach in which oral media and aural techniques have an essential place alongside manual media.

Holland has had a reputation for its pure oralism, due largely to the work of the St. Michielsgestel School at Eindhoven, but even there, changes have occurred. At the St. Michielsgestel School itself, children who are not considered to be capable of making good progress through pure oral education are taught by a combined method using fingerspelling with speech and lipreading (Van Uden, 1974).

It has been suggested by Tervoort (Note 6) that the home training programs set up in Holland in the late 1950s, to encourage mothers to use speech and to avoid gestural communication, were of limited success in facilitating future speech development. He records that

there grew more and more doubt about the acceptability of such a drastic intervention in the vital first interactions between mother and child. There was growing conviction that the demands of the subsequent speech education were exaggerated . . . so the question arose if it would not be much better afterall not to interfere in this first interaction in signs (p. 4).

Tervoort argued that normally the use of "all modalities is a matter of natural course at the beginning of life between mother and child." He supported the concept of total communication as a selective process, which emphasizes the use of oral or manual media, or both, according to individual needs.

As far as communication with the deaf child is concerned . . . the most efficient modality or modalities in each case should be preferred. Usually that will be a combinatory form. Intensive use of all residual functional hearing is included as explicitly as the use of manual signs, but he who has to make out without the first or can do without the second modality still uses total communication (p. 10).

These views of an eminent linguist reflect the wide acceptance of the total communication concept and the growing understanding of its relevance to language acquisition.

In countries in other parts of the world, there has been acceptance of total communication. In Malaysia, the Federation School for the Deaf at Penang was originally founded on pure oral principles, but eventual dissatisfaction with the results obtained led to a change. Following extensive study of developments in the United States and Britain, the principal of the school introduced a combined approach to teaching (Isa, Note 7). The philosophy of total communication has also influenced practice in Jamaica (Campbell, Note 8) and in Costa Rica (Campos, Note 9).

In Australia, there was, in the past, less extreme difference of educational opinion than in the United States and some European countries and a coexistence between schools using pure oral teaching and schools using combined methods. According to an Australian educator (Jeanes, Note 10), by the close of the 1970s, all of the states had a major school practicing total communication, complementing the work done for a proportion of hearing-impaired children educated in ordinary schools. The general approach in these schools is to use a manual representation of English based upon the lexicon of Australian Sign Language in conjunction with oral communication.

Total communication has evolved as a liberal attitude toward the use of appropriate media to meet individual needs or different situations, rather than a precise way of teaching. It has been emphasized that total communication is a philosophy, not a method. But philosophy alone does not guarantee more successful or satisfying results; attainments in education are influenced more directly by teaching method. The philosophy advocates *what* media should be available; *how* they should be used is a matter of methodology. Total communication, as a philosophy, has to be implemented in practice. The next chapter looks, in broad terms, at the way in which total communication as a concept has developed in educational practice. This provides a foundation for more detailed consideration, in the later chapters, of the theoretical issues that might determine appropriate methodology.

The previous chapter looked at the origin of the contemporary philosophy of total communication as an educational movement. It considered the research evidence which suggested the need for change, both the negative evidence of results of the pure oral approach and the positive evidence of the efficiency of combined media communication. The chapter traced the development of the new eclectic attitude which advocated the use of oral and manual media and the spreading influence of this attitude from the United States to other countries.

The discussions have described what the total communication philosophy is, but the ultimate need is to understand how total communication might be used to influence actual teaching and planning for language growth. This will be the main concern of the remainder of the book. This chapter attempts to span the gap between broad philosophy and more detailed ideas of methodology by examining developments in practice. It provides some information on how widely total communication has been established and reports observations on actual practice at some schools.

THE GROWTH IN PRACTICE   From the time that total communication was formally introduced into educational practice there has been a steady acceptance in the United States. Garretson (1976) carried out a preliminary inquiry which revealed that, during the period from 1968 to 1976, this approach had been adopted by an average of ten schools a year.

In the academic year 1975–76, a thorough survey of communication methods used for hearing-impaired children in schools and classes throughout the United States was conducted by Jordan, Gustason, and Rosen (1976). For the purpose of their questionnaire survey, they defined four main "methods" as follows:

1) Oral/Aural—the use of amplification and speechreading without manual cues. 2) Rochester—the use of fingerspelling in conjunction with speechreading and amplification. 3) Total Communication—the use of manual signs, fingerspelling, speechreading and amplification. 4) Cued Speech—the system of hand cues utilized with speech for speechreading (p. 527).

The results of their survey indicated that considerable change had occurred in communication practice. Of the 796 programs (i.e., schools or classes) responding, 43 percent reported a recent change in their practice, and this was particularly the case at preschool and elementary levels. The trend was away from pure oral methods and toward total communication. A significant finding was that 308 programs offered, or participated in, instruction in signing to hearing-impaired students. This was in contrast to the virtual lack of formal instruction in signing reported by Falberg (1964) for the previous decade.

The authors of the study pointed out that, this being an area of rapid change, the details of the situation might well quickly become outdated. Two years later, a follow-up survey was carried out (Jordan, Gustason, and Rosen, 1979) which provided new information on practices in schools up to the academic year 1977–78. The 642 schools or classes responding represented a combined population of 31,285 students in 5,229 classes. It is important to note that a substantial proportion of these students, 37 percent of the total, were in mainstreamed classes.

The results revealed that 77 percent of all the programs had made a change in their communication practice during the ten-year period 1968 to 1978. The analysis of year-by-year changes indicated that the trend toward total communication had been substantial and was leveling off by 1978. At that time, nearly 65 percent of the classes responding to the survey used total communication as defined by the authors. This figure contrasted with nearly 35 percent using a pure oral method. The Rochester method of fingerspelling with speech was used in 0.5 percent and Cued Speech in 0.2 percent of the classes.

The survey also inquired about the signing or sign language textbooks used as sources of reference. From the information obtained, it was inferred that, within the total communication programs, there was a growing trend toward some form of systematic signing of English, particularly with preschool and elementary children. One important related finding was that most of the programs had given attention to the problem of internal standardization and consistent use of signs within schools and had already reached a solution or were actively working in pursuit of one. (These different forms of signing and the systems referred to in the following section are defined and explained in Chapter 5.) Among the textbooks reported, manual English or signed English systems held prominent place, but instructional textbooks for sign language or for signing in simultaneous communication were also represented.

One of the authors of these American surveys subsequently made a similar study of communication trends in the United Kingdom. Jordan (Note 11), working from Edinburgh, inquired into methods of communication used in schools in Great Britain and Northern Ireland during the academic year 1980–81. A total of 54 (or 72 percent of) special schools for deaf children and 346 (or 71 percent of) partially hearing units in ordinary schools responded to his questionnaire survey. This represented a total of 7,569 pupils, 3,808 in schools for deaf children and 3,761 in partially hearing units.

The results indicated that 54 percent of the schools reported the use of manual media to some extent; but as pure oral teaching was used with some children within schools, a more accurate picture might be gained from the examination of individual classes. At the primary level (up to the age of about twelve years), 40 percent of classes were taught through total communication, and at the secondary level, the figure was 35 percent. The trend toward total communication had commenced in the early 1970s, and most of the changes had occurred during the two-year period from 1979 to 1981.

Units in ordinary schools were originally set up to provide for partially hearing children who, almost by definition, might be expected to progress in speech and language development through oral teaching. There has, however, been some tendency to place severely deaf children in such units, and it is significant that Jordan ascertained some use of combined oral and manual media. By 1981, 9 percent of classes in primary units and 7 percent of classes in secondary units were using total communication, and further units were considering which form of signing to introduce—from British Sign Language, Sign-English, and Paget-Gorman Sign System. In addition, while not adopting the full concept of total communication, some units supplemented oral teaching with fingerspelling or Cued Speech.

DEVELOPMENTS IN SCHOOLS   These studies provided a good picture of the broad pattern of communication trends; but, of course, they were not specifically studies of total communication, and, as questionnaire surveys, they did not attempt description of practices within individual schools. Some information on the way in which total communication has developed in schools helps in the consideration of the more detailed aspects of teaching methodology and the problems involved in its implementation. The remaining part of this chapter reports a study carried out to provide some such information.

Observations were made during the early part of 1981 in eight American schools known to have adopted the philosophy of total communication (Evans, Note 12). The length of experience of total communication within individual schools ranged from five to twelve years. Whereas the surveys, already referred to, provide a broad picture, the aim of these observations in a small number of schools was to identify some emerging ideas and problems. In particular, it was important to ask which media are used and with which children; more specifically, what ideas have emerged on the place of sign language or signing of English; and what are the experiences in the training of teachers and parents in new skills.

These schools had in common the use of Sign-English as a main language form, the signs of sign language used in the syntactic order of English words. In two schools, the work with the youngest children was based upon the Signed English system and teaching materials (Bornstein, Hamilton, and Saulnier, 1975). Two other schools, when changing to a total communication approach, had first adopted Signing Exact English (Gustason, Pfetzing, and Zawolkow, 1972) but had quite quickly changed to a more natural use of Sign-English. One school had originally introduced Cued Speech, as its first move from a pure oral tradition; this was not sustained, and in due course, total communication was adopted as the official policy, using Sign-English as the form of signing. American Sign Language was also recognized in them and tended to be used socially by older students—in effect a bilingual situation.

Two interesting observations were made about the place of sign language in teaching. At one school, it had been noted that after using Sign-English to lay down syntactic rules of English, when a stage of more rapid building up of new vocabulary was reached, the students tended to move toward sign language structure. At another school, it was considered that sign language was particularly helpful for learning of new content and concepts in subjects such as mathematics and science which were later "restructured" in English syntax, including fingerspelling.

A significant report from the schools was that fingerspelling could be used with young children from the time they first entered school and certainly before the age of three years. Fingerspelling was usually introduced concurrently with early signing. Fingerspelled words were learned as "signs," or contractions, at first, before formal attention was given to written language.

These schools viewed total communication as involving the use of both oral and manual media. Specialized services were devoted to audiological support, and attention was given to the teaching of speech. In general, speech and signing were developed concurrently. It is noteworthy that most schools used the scheme devised by Dr. Daniel Ling (1976) for the systematic development of speech skills.

A major preoccupation was the work with additionally handicapped children who accounted for up to 25 percent of the places at individual schools. Total communication was proving to be of special relevance to the needs of these children. Actual communication techniques were modified according to the needs of different disabilities. The most general observation was one of greater emphasis upon conceptual signs rather than full syntactic structures with slow learning children.

Much importance was attached to the instruction of parents and teachers in manual communication skills. Considerable progress had been made in the in-service training of teachers, and at least two schools formally required, for continuing employment, that teachers and other members of staff acquire working proficiency in manual communication within an appropriate period of time.

The training of parents presented a more difficult problem. Success varied with the differing levels of willingness and aptitude for instruction. The estimates of the proportion of parents attaining competence in signing ranges from 25 percent to 50 percent. This highlights the difficulty, but there was a hopeful indication at one school. Whereas only about 10 percent of parents of older students, who had been brought up under a pure oral approach, gained competence in signing, about 80 percent of new parents learning signing at the same time as their young children in the parent-infant program became proficient.

Although these observations were centered upon special schools, there was some information of relevance to developments in ordinary schools. Two of the schools had mainstreaming programs. Some children were able to be transferred into ordinary schools with the support of total communication. This included direct teaching in simultaneous communication, or the interpretation of lessons by visiting tutors.

Finally, there was one interesting example of "reverse integration" of hearing children into a school for the deaf. The special school had a popular preschool nursery program with a majority of hearing children attending part-time and just a few deaf children in each class. This mixed group was conducted through total communication with mutual benefits. The deaf children were exposed to the predominant normal language environment and stimulus to speech, and the hearing children learned manual communication skills.

These observations, at a small number of schools, do not allow broad generalizations. They do, however, provide insights into some salient features of actual developments in total communication practice. These form a useful framework of reference for interpreting research findings and assessing their relevance to teaching methodology. Before considering such theoretical issues, however, it will be necessary first to take account of the actual component parts of total communication, the oral and manual media themselves. This is done in the following chapters.

In order to understand the nature and scope of total communication, it is necessary first to understand its constituent parts. In order to assess the value of the different media, it is necessary to know something of their linguistic qualities. It should be asked whether they are themselves languages or codes for transmitting language, and whether they contribute to language acquisition or are of use mainly for subsequent language communication. With these questions in mind, the main linguistic media involved in total communication can be considered.

In people with normal hearing, one usually thinks of expression and reception of speech—speaking, or articulation, and hearing, or listening. For deaf people, one must also consider the additional "special" aspect—visual reception of speech by lipreading. This chapter deals with speech and lipreading. The main manual media, fingerspelling and signing, are examined in the following chapters. Research is reviewed that helps the understanding of the formational properties and perceptual parameters of these systems and tells something about their communicative efficiency and developmental effects with deaf children.

In practice, these systems are intended to represent spoken language (or its written form), or to act as a substitute or supplement for spoken language. These different media are discussed in relation to English, but it is important to realize that there might be some differences in relation to other spoken languages.

SPEECH A principal tenet of the oral philosophy is that speech, as the natural language medium in hearing children, should also be the medium for language acquisition, communication, and learning in deaf children. Total communication also places high value on speech, but in combination with additional forms of communication.

Partially hearing, or hard of hearing, children with substantial residual hearing might be capable of developing speech and language largely along natural lines by hearing and imitating the speech around them. Thus, they should be able to benefit from pure oral education. As we are not specifically concerned with such children, detailed aspects of aural reception of speech will not be dealt with here. A proper understanding of the background to hearing loss and the stimulation of residual hearing through auditory amplification and training should be more appropriately gained from textbooks in the well-established field of audiology.

This study of total communication is concerned with children who need access to manual communication because they cannot understand speech adequately through hearing. The discussion of speech will be centered on the problems of expressive speech and the visual reception of speech through lipreading.

Little detailed objective study has been done of the expressive speech of deaf children. The available evidence from research simply confirmed that deaf children had immense difficulty in acquiring speech and that only a small proportion of children with severe congenital hearing loss attained expressive *intelligibility*, that is, speech that could be easily understood by others.

The evidence of an objective survey, from an impeccable source, the Department of Education and Science (1964), provided a picture of the speech of hearing-impaired adolescents in British schools at a time when priority was given to education through oral communication. The conversational speech of the children was graded, by the same assessor throughout, into intelligible, partly intelligible, and unintelligible categories. Of those children with mean hearing losses in excess of 80 decibels, more than 88 percent had speech that was not wholly intelligible; about 45 percent had speech rated as partly intelligible, although, in most cases, not likely to be understood by people unfamiliar with deaf children.

In another British study, Markides (1970) recorded the spontaneous speech of deaf and partially hearing children. Lay persons unfamiliar with deaf children listened to the recordings and reported the words they understood. For the deaf children, more than 80 percent of the words were not correctly recognized. Of all the children, deaf and partially hearing, about two-thirds had speech which was either unintelligible or very difficult to follow.

A similar effect was reported in an American study. Levitt (1976) recorded the speech of deaf adolescents who were asked to describe verbally short picture sequences. The speech of about 75 percent of the subjects was graded as either unintelligible or very difficult to understand. In a more extensive study, Jensema, Karchmer, and Trybus (1978) obtained teacher ratings for nearly 1,000 hearing-impaired children. They analyzed the results by degree of hearing loss. Of the profoundly deaf children with mean hearing losses in excess of 90 decibels, 77 percent had speech that was unintelligible or just barely intelligible; of the severely deaf with hearing losses between 70 and 90 decibels, 45 percent had such speech; for those children with hearing losses less than 70 decibels, the corresponding figure was 14 percent.

In a detailed, experimental study, Conrad (1979) had the speech of 331 British children graded by teachers on the basis of how easily people unfamiliar with deaf children would be expected to understand. He also analyzed his results by hearing loss. Of the moderately deaf children with hearing losses below 65 decibels, less than 10 percent had speech which was graded as unintelligible or very hard to understand, but of the most profoundly deaf group with hearing losses exceeding 105 decibels, the figure was 85 percent.

These findings are, of themselves, in no way startling; deafness is an obvious barrier to acquisition of speech. But some significance lies in the possible effect that expressive speech ability might have upon the capacity to internalize speech. It is believed that internal speech is important for thinking. Conrad (1971) demonstrated that, in hearing children, vocal speech precedes internal speech. He concluded that his findings with deaf children supported the hypothesis that speech intelligibility in deaf children determines the extent of useful internal speech, independently of hearing loss and intelligence.

Internal speech is demonstrably a valuable cognitive tool. It appears to be highly dependent on the presence of intelligible speech. Not only therefore is good vocal speech of immense value in the broader sense, but it evidently provides a means by which children can communicate with themselves (p. 230).

Conrad also proposed that internal speech is important for lipreading development (and this will be discussed further in the following section). It could be argued that, even if speech is not externally intelligible, it might be meaningful to the child, and its consistent use might still act as internal reinforcement of thought.

From these findings, two important implications for teaching methodology can be deduced. As speech intelligibility is important for internal speech development, which itself facilitates thinking and contributes to lipreading, speech training should have an appropriate place in any method of teaching deaf children. In view of the tendency for the more severely deaf children to be less likely to develop adequate internal speech, and in considering the use of additional special forms of communication, we should give regard to the possibility that these might be internalized to promote cognitive activity—"internal fingerspelling" and "internal signing." McGuigan (Note 13) carried out an interesting experiment which throws some light on this possibility. Electromyographic recordings (to detect covert muscle action) were made for deaf adults while read-ing silently, thinking, or doing mental arithmetic prob-lems. The deaf subjects who used signing were found to send signals to the arm muscles, in the way that hearing subjects send signals to the speech muscles when proces-sing language information.

LIPREADING   A severely deaf person is unable to hear speech but might understand what is said by watching the speaker's face. It is possible to perceive spoken language through *lipreading*, which involves visual perception of the shapes and movements made in normal articulation of speech sounds. In the comprehension of spoken language, use is made of facial and linguistic cues, and the alternative term *speechreading* is an appropriate description of this process. However, as lipreading is a universal term, and the more widely used term outside the United States, we shall use it here.

Visual reception of speech through lipreading is less complete and accurate than the corresponding auditory re-ception of speech with normal hearing. The main factors which influence lipreading of continuous speech are the re-strictive visual characteristics of speech sounds, and the compensating use of linguistic cues which can help to off-set these restraints.

The speech sounds of continuous spoken language are audible to a person with normal hearing in suitable condi-tions, but the shapes and movements that are produced in articulation of speech vary in their degree of visibility. Some sounds, such as [k] and [g] are virtually unidentifiable as visual elements. Markides (1977), from his review of American studies of lipreading, concluded that the speech sounds fall along a continuum of visibility with the vowels being more visible and the consonants less visible. Unfor-tunately, as far as English is concerned, the more fre-quently occurring speech sounds happen to be the least vis-ible on the lips, and the most visible are the more rarely used sounds (Jeffers and Barley, 1971).

There is also a problem of visual similarity. Some of the speech sounds, although visible, have similar shapes, such as the voiced and unvoiced pair of consonants [d] and [t]. These visually indistinguishable speech sounds or, "look-alikes," have been termed *homophenes*. The acoustically distinct speech sounds of English cluster into a smaller number of visually similar, or homophenous, groups. There is not a simple one-to-one correspondence between the speech sounds and their distinctive lipread shapes.

Work by Woodward and Lowell (1964) and Berger (1972) suggests that vowel sounds, although more identifiable in isolation, become less distinctive in continuous speech. Fisher (1968) classified vowels into four main groups, while Wolff (1971) suggested only three broad groups of lipshapes for vowels.

Extensive studies of consonants have revealed a similar discrimination problem (Bruhn, 1942; Burchett, 1950; Clegg, 1953; Berger, 1972; Binnie, Jackson, and Montgomery, 1976). Experimental work by Woodward and Barber (1960) suggests that the consonants fall into four main groups, which can be described broadly as: (1) bilabial [p,b,m]; (2) rounded labial [w,r]; (3) labio-dental [f,v]; and (4) nonlabial (comprising the remaining consonants). This analysis has been supported by similar experimental work by Woodward and Lowell (1964), Fisher (1968), and Walden, Prosek, and Worthington (1974).

The estimates of the number of such groupings varies, but it is clear that a problem of reduced visual reception of speech sounds exists. Hardy (1970) suggests that over two-thirds of English speech sounds are either invisible or visually indistinguishable from at least one other. According to Eggermont (cited in Lenneberg, 1967, p. 321), even the most proficient lipreaders cannot identify more than 40 to 50 percent of speech sounds. These homophenous speech sounds, in turn, combine to produce words which look alike for lipreading (for example, *mate* and *paid*). Estimates of the proportion of homophenous words in English range from 40 to 60 percent (Bruhn, 1949; Wood and Blakely, 1953; Vernon and Mindel, 1971). In isolation, such words cannot be distinguished purely visually; in lipreading of continuous speech, they have to be differentiated by using linguistic cues from the context of the discourse. Experimental confirmation of this was provided by Erber and Mc-Mahon (1976) in their study of the effects of sentence context on recognition of words through lipreading by deaf children; they concluded that relatively high levels of linguistic knowledge are necessary before context can aid lipreading.

When this point is understood, it should not be surprising that hearing people with normal language tend to score as well as, or better than, deaf people on tests of lipreading with understanding (Di Carlo and Kataja, 1951; Lowell, 1959; Butt and Chreist, 1968; Berger, 1972). In a British study, Conrad (1979) found that deaf school leavers with at least ten years experience of lipreading did not perform better on lipreading tests than inexperienced hearing children.

The need to understand speech through lipreading goes with deafness, and increasing deafness imposes greater need; but the research findings indicate that actual lipreading ability in deaf children tends to decrease with severity of hearing loss. In an American study, Simmons (1959) found a negative correlation between hearing loss and lipreading ability. Inverse relationships were confirmed in a series of British studies (Evans, 1960, 1965, 1978). In spite of greater need, more severely deaf children tend to have lower lipreading levels than moderately deaf children. Their more limited language development can partly explain this; lipreading as a code for receiving spoken language cannot exceed the level of competence in that language.

But Conrad (1979) has shown that this is not the complete explanation. He found a significant negative relationship between increasing hearing loss and speech comprehension through lipreading, but pointed out that this "in itself tells us little more than that children with more hearing also understand more spoken language" (p. 180). By making a further analysis, restricted to the material that the children could actually read, he was able to examine lipreading performance as a ratio of actual linguistic knowledge. He found that there was still an inverse correlation, and concluded that the more severely deaf children have lower understanding through lipreading, "not just because they know less language; they also lipread less of what they do know" (p. 187). Savage et al. (1981) also demonstrated, through the higher levels of understanding English syntax by fingerspelling and signing, that lipreading fails to reach actual level of linguistic competence in English. To find explanations of this, it is necessary to look further at the influence of perceptual and cognitive factors.

Experimental studies of the influence of visual perceptual variables upon lipreading performance have produced little positive evidence. Early American studies reported lack of relationship between lipreading attainment and tests of visual spatial ability (O'Neill, 1951), visual recognition (O'Neill and Davidson, 1956), and visual memory (Simmons, 1959). A British study found lipreading performance to have no correlation with visual acuity but a moderate relationship with visual memory for nonverbal designs (Evans, 1965).

The relationship between lipreading and intelligence has received more extensive attention, but with rather discrepant results. In the earliest study, Pintner (1929) concluded that, beyond a very low level of ability, intelligence does not influence lipreading ability. Farwell (1976), in a research review, records that most studies yielded low positive, but not significant, correlations. As linguistic knowledge enhances lipreading potential, and if general intelligence contributes to language development, we might expect to find an indirect association between intelligence and lipreading. An examination of studies reporting lack of significant correlation shows that these were, in the main, based upon tests of basic visual recognition rather than comprehension of the information (Reid, 1947; O'Neill and Davidson, 1956; Simmons, 1959; Butt and Chreist, 1968; Quigley, 1969; Lewis, 1972). In studies designed to test understanding of language through lipreading, intelligence was found to have significant moderate influence (Evans, 1965, 1978). Craig (1964), Montgomery (1966, 1968, and 1976), Neyhus (1969), and Quigley (1969) also reported significant correlations between lipreading and intelligence.

Conrad (1979) reported significant moderate correlations for groups of subjects with varying levels of hearing loss. As he had done in his treatment of hearing loss and intelligence, he made a further analysis of the ratio of lipreading performance to actual linguistic knowledge which confirmed the significant correlation. Conrad's is a particularly valuable study which leads to the conclusion that, in addition to the contribution to lipreading through its influence on language development, intelligence enables children to make better use of their knowledge of the language of the test. Conrad pointed out, however, that the actual level of correlations was too low to be of much predictive value and that this, together with the other evidence, "suggests that lip reading is a skill which is likely to be difficult to teach formally" (p. 193).

The correlations which have been reported in the research—hearing loss related to lipreading, and intelligence related to lipreading—have been explained in terms of the probable indirect relationship that they exert through their influence upon language development. If this is the case, we should expect there to be a direct relationship between language development and lipreading. A British study examined this question (Evans, 1978). A group of sixty-five deaf children, aged between eleven and seventeen years, were asked to lipread a language reception test and were also given the Group Reading Test devised by Young (1968). There was a significant correlation between the *internal speech?*

results of these two tests (r=0.49, p<.001). The possible indirect influence of hearing loss and intelligence upon lipreading through language development has already been explained. When the effects of these two variables were controlled, the resultant partial correlation (r=0.38, p<.001) indicated a still significant direct relationship between reading ability and lipreading comprehension.

Conrad (1979) also proposed a relationship between internal speech and lipreading. Reference has been made to his detailed experimental findings on internal speech. Children with less severe hearing loss are more likely to have intelligible speech; children with intelligible vocal speech are more likely to have internal speech. It had been suggested, by Myklebust (1964) in the United States and also by Dodd (1977) in Britain, that lipreading is necessary for the development of internal speech. But Conrad, from his experimental results, argued that internal speech is one of the main contributors, with residual hearing and intelligence, to lipreading.

CUED SPEECH   For profoundly deaf children, the combined use of residual hearing and lipreading fails to reach a level of speech reception comparable to normal hearing. Dr. Orin Cornett devised a system known as *Cued Speech* to clarify the ambiguities of lipreading by providing supplementary information on the hands. The system uses twelve hand shapes which, in combination with the lip shapes, provide a one-to-one correspondence with the phonemes of spoken language. For example, the visually contrastive consonants [t,m,f] share the same manual cue, but conversely the visually similar consonants [p,b,m] have different hand cues. As the cues only identify groups of vowels and consonants which are internally contrasted visually, they do not in themselves give complete recognition of speech. The system supplements, rather than replaces, information on the lips and therefore is regarded as an oral system of communication (Cornett, 1967).

Cues for Southern English Vowels

	Group I (base position)	Group II (larynx)	Group III (chin)	Group IV (mouth)
open	[a :] (fäther)	[a] (thăt)	[ŏ] (pot)	[ŭ] (but)
flattened-relaxed	[δ :] (her) (fur)	[i] (ĭs)	[e] (gĕt)	[i :] (feet) (meat)
rounded	[ou] (nōte) (boat)	[u] (good) (put)	[u :] (blue) (food)	[o :] (for) (ought)
neutral	[a] (mother)			

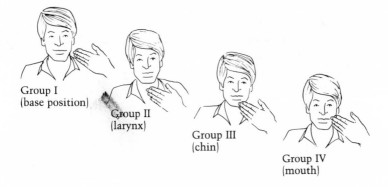

Group I (base position)

Group II (larynx)

Group III (chin)

Group IV (mouth)

Cues for English Consonants

T Group*	H Group	D Group	ng Group	L Group	K Group	N Group	G Group
t	h	d	(ng)	l	k	n	g
m	s	p	y (you)	sh	v	b	j
f	r	zh	ch	w	th (the)	hw	th (thin)
					z		

* Note: The T group cue is also with an isolated vowel—that is, an initial vowel not run in with a final consonant from the preceding syllable.

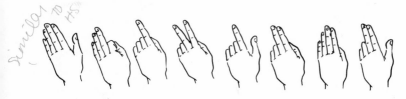

Figure 5. The hand shapes of Cued Speech

Cued Speech is not the first such attempt to use a manual system to resolve the visual ambiguities of lipreading. The *Mouth-Hand* system, invented by Dr. Georg Forchhammer (1903), gained practical usage in Denmark. This system also used hand formations to identify the visual ambiguities of speech sounds.

During the late nineteenth century, an attempt had been made to produce a complete manual code to represent all speech sounds. Edmund Lyon, who was familiar with fingerspelling as used at the Rochester School for the Deaf, first devised a system based upon shorthand symbols. Later, he became influenced by *Visible Speech*, the system invented by Alexander Melville Bell, father of Alexander Graham Bell. Visible Speech comprised graphic symbols representing the articulatory movements of speech (A.M. Bell, 1895). Lyon's *Phonetic Finger Alphabet* attempted to represent these symbols manually. As there was a total of 120 hand formations, this system did not attain lasting practical popularity (Scouten, 1942).

Perhaps an even earlier antecedent of Cued Speech was Pereire's dactylology, an augmentation of the manual alphabet to represent phonetic qualities of spoken French.

In developing Cued Speech, Cornett was able to take account of such experimental data as the visual contrast of speech sounds (Woodward and Barber, 1960) and their statistical frequency of occurrence (Denes, 1963). Experimental studies of the practical efficiency of Cued Speech have been limited. A small study by Ling and Clarke (1975) in Canada tested deaf children who had been introduced to Cued Speech following failure by earlier pure oral education. The speech recognition score for these children by Cued Speech (12 percent) was better than pure lipreading (6 percent), but they considered the overall performance to be low. A follow-up study one year later (Clarke and Ling, 1976) found a substantial improvement in recognition both with and without cues, and they concluded that Cued

Speech clarified the lipread information. In another small study, Nicholls (1979) tested Australian children who had used Cued Speech for at least four years, some of whom had earlier use of fingerspelling or signing. Nicholls concluded that her results supported the claim that Cued Speech enabled profoundly deaf children to receive relatively precise phonemic and linguistic information, and that the use of cues with lipreading enabled these deaf children to achieve high levels of perception of words in sentences. Again, an association was found between speech perception through Cued Speech and language attainment.

Lipreading, as the receptive medium in oral communication, is a means by which deaf people may receive and understand the normal speech of hearing people. The other means of "live" visual communication of language available to deaf people involve systems which require special skills on the part of both sender and receiver. These systems are characterized by the use of gestures or movements made by the hands and are known as *manual media* of communication. The two broad kinds of manual media to be discussed are signing and fingerspelling. As fingerspelling is used in some forms of signing, it will be helpful to first deal with fingerspelling before going on to explain the different forms of signing in the following chapter.

It is possible to transmit written language on the hands. This is done by *fingerspelling*, which uses hand and finger shapes to represent the alphabetic letters of written language. As there is one-to-one equivalence between the manual symbols and the graphic symbols, fingerspelling has word-for-word correspondence with reading and writing. The term covers both reception and expression, so that it is necessary to distinguish between these aspects by referring to fingerspelling production, or "sending," and fingerspelling reception, or "reading."

MANUAL ALPHABETS There are many forms of fingerspelling, or *manual alphabets*, in use throughout different countries. These fall into two main types known as *one-handed* alphabets and *two-handed* alphabets.

Manual alphabets are believed to have existed and to have been used more generally by hearing people before they were applied in teaching deaf people. Members of silent religious orders used such means for communication, and several forms were known to be used in England as early as the eighth century. The one-handed manual alphabet of twenty-two "letters" used in the early education of deaf people in Spain was published by Bonet in 1620. An expanded version, to represent written French, was used by the Spaniard Pereire when he began teaching in France in the early eighteenth century. This became established as part of the French method of teaching developed by de l'Epée. The American, Thomas Hopkins Gallaudet, learned this method of teaching from Sicard at Paris. When he returned to the United States accompanied by the Frenchman Clerc to set up the school for the deaf in Connecticut in 1817, he included the one-handed form of fingerspelling in the teaching method. This one-handed system continued to be used in the United States and, in its current form, is generally known as the American Manual Alphabet.

In Great Britain, and in some countries that were historically linked with Britain, a two-handed form of fingerspelling is used. The origin of this goes back to the manual alphabet illustrated in an anonymous pamphlet, *Digiti Lingua*, which was published in London in 1698. There is some use of one-handed fingerspelling in Britain, including the formal introduction of the American Manual Alphabet into teaching methods in a school for deaf children.

There are also some "mixed" manual alphabets. Examples of these are the traditional systems of Yugoslavia and Italy, both of which include some one-handed and some two-handed formations.

The World Federation of the Deaf, at its International Congress held at Stockholm in 1963, decided to adopt the American system as the basis for an international manual alphabet (with a modification being made for the letter [T], as this was also a sign with dubious acceptability in some European countries). There has been something of a trend toward a standardized use of this one-handed alphabet. For instance, the deaf people of Denmark had their own traditional one-handed form of fingerspelling, which was also used in Norway due to the close historical ties of the two

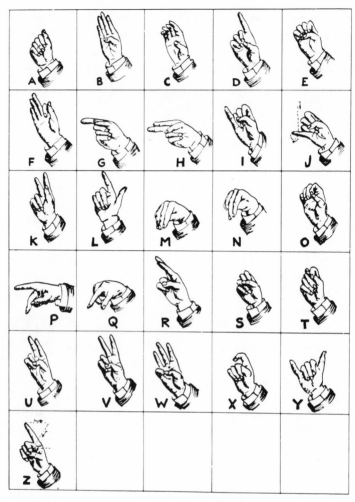

Figure 6. The American one-handed manual alphabet

countries. Norway adopted the international manual alphabet in 1963, with three additional formations for the extra letters of the Norwegian written alphabet. Denmark made a formal acceptance of the international manual alphabet for the World Federation of the Deaf Conference at Copenhagen in 1977. The one-handed alphabet has also been adopted in some countries where fingerspelling was introduced into teaching method for the first time, such as in Malaysia.

Fingerspelling can also be used for tactile communication with people who are both deaf and blind. The British

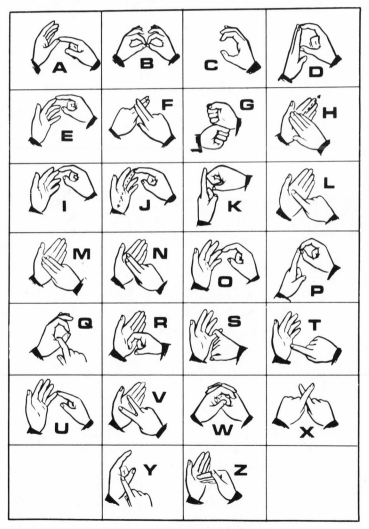

Figure 7. The British two-handed manual alphabet

Manual Alphabet, being two-handed, can be used in a modified form in which the sender makes the right hand move-

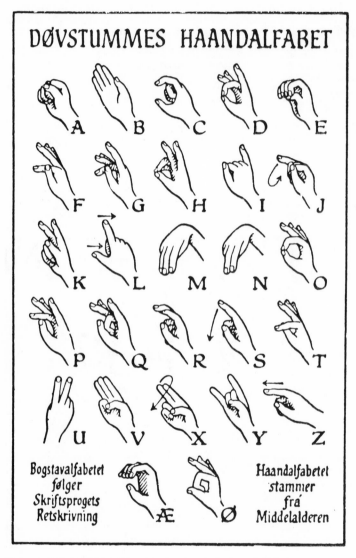

Figure 8. The traditional Danish one-handed manual alphabet

ments against the left hand of the reader. An invented system, the Lorm Deaf-Blind Manual Alphabet, has been used in some European countries and also in the United States. The sender's hand moves across the hand of the receiver—touching, moving, or squeezing one or more fingers of the right hand.

There are also a variety of manual systems for indicating quantity. Anderson (1980), who made a detailed analysis of European systems, came to the interesting conclusion that the handshapes of the fingerspelling alphabet originated in the hand numbers of sign languages. He explained that the three simplest counting systems start from the thumb, the index finger, and the little finger, and then proceed in order along the fingers. From Figure 9 it can be seen that there are, in relation to just the American Manual Alphabet, several handshapes which correspond to fingerspelling formations for letters, viz., [A, with extended thumb; L; W, extended; D; V; W; I; and F]. Further, the formations for [5], which is common to all these systems, and for [3] are recognized handshapes of sign language (as will be explained in the following chapter on signing).

THE FINGERSPELLING PROCESS   Fingerspelling has not received as much attention as lipreading, but there have been some experimental studies to help our understanding of the process. These can be examined in terms of some perceptual parameters and individual differences.

The individual hand shapes, or *formations*, of fingerspelling combine in temporal sequences into *configurations* which represent words of written language in continuous discourse. Experimental work by Hanson (1980) has produced evidence to suggest that fingerspelling occurs at a level of whole word perception. She asked deaf adults skilled in manual communication to watch and write down the words produced by skilled fingerspellers. Three types of "words" were used: (a) English words (for example, *vehicle, advertisement*); (b) pseudowords, which were not

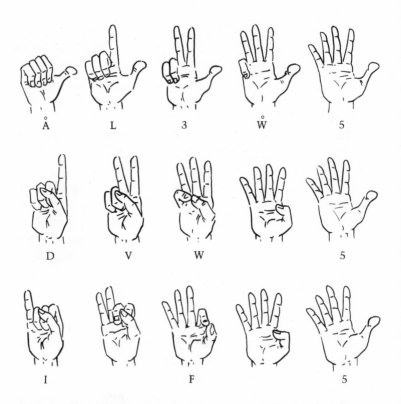

Figure 9. Three different manual counting systems showing the relationship with American one-handed alphabet formations

actual English words but obeyed the spelling rules in English (for example, *mungrats, brandigan*); and (c) nonwords, which violated English spelling and could not be English words (for example, *fternaps, vetmftern*). The subjects of the study were most successful in correctly writing the English words and least successful in writing the nonwords, a result which was consistent with the findings of general experiments for the graphic reading of such materials. Hanson took this as evidence that reading of fingerspelling is not a process of identifying individual letters but rather of recognizing whole visual configurations.

This principle might be central to the efficient learning of the skill of fingerspelling. Levitt and Groode (1980) observed that in children learning to fingerspell, reception precedes expression. They take this into account in their approach to teaching fingerspelling to adults. They emphasize the importance of practice in the initial recognition of overall configurations of whole words.

Fingerspelling is a code for transmitting written language. Written language is itself a code, or secondary medium, based upon spoken language as the primary medium in which original language competence is acquired; thus, fingerspelling may be thought of as a tertiary, or third level, code, which is usually learned from written language. This leads to the question of how it is stored in short-term memory. Is fingerspelling coded in the same or a different category to written language?

There has been some relevant work by Hoemann (1978) that throws light upon this problem. He carried out some experiments with deaf subjects, based upon what has been called the "proactive interference" effect in short-term memory. Earlier work (with hearing subjects) by Wickens, Born, and Allen (1963) had established that in the course of successive trials of short-term memorizing of graphic letters of the alphabet, recall performance deteriorates due to the interference in remembering new material from the similar material already being stored in memory. This is termed proactive inhibition. When the test items are changed from alphabetic letters to numeral digits, recall improves due to the "release" from the proactive inhibition. This is taken as evidence that the two types of stimuli are coded separately in short-term memory.

In Hoemann's study, deaf college students were presented written alphabetic letters for three successive trials; then, a switch was made to fingerspelled formations. With a second group, the procedure was reversed, the switch being made from manual alphabetic to graphic alphabetic symbols. In both cases, there was initial deterioration in recall, consistent with the proactive interference effect, but an improvement with the change of material. Two control groups of subjects were given the same type of material throughout, with no switch for their fourth trial, and they had no recovery effect. The results were also in contrast to a control task, in which the switch was made from upper to lower case graphic letters and which produced no release of proactive inhibition. From these results, Hoemann concluded that fingerspelled and written alphabetic symbols of English are coded in separate categories in short-term memory by deaf people. Hoemann considered this to be evidence that the American Manual Alphabet, although derived from its alphabetic representation of English letters, is not merely a code for English but a part of the manual communication system used by deaf people in North America.

Further support for the view of the American Manual Alphabet as an integral feature of American Sign Language is offered in the findings of a study of the different error patterns of deaf children's fingerspelling and spelling of written English. A far higher proportion of errors of fingerspelling were accounted for by omissions. Hoemann (p. 303) suggests that fingerspelling is acquired primarily as a means of communication rather than as a way to spell English and, as such, has a tolerance level for missing information to meet the demands of ordinary conversation.

A popular criticism of fingerspelling is that it might be difficult to read at a distance, such as the rear of a school assembly hall or auditorium. But, as a substitute for hearing of speech and as an alternative to lipreading alone, fingerspelling should be evaluated in similar conditions to those in which normal speech can be received. Some information is available on the reception of fingerspelling at a distance from the sender. In an experimental study of this problem (Moser et al., 1958), deaf students were able to re-

ceive nonmeaningful fingerspelled material with almost 90
percent intelligibility at a distance of 125 feet. Students
rated as good were able to achieve this level of accuracy up
to 175 feet.

It is a well-known fact that people differ widely in the
clarity of their handwriting or how intelligible it appears to
other people as readers. There are also variations in the
fingerspelling intelligibility of different people. Fisher and
Husa (1973) asked ten people, including five deaf and five
hearing, all experienced in using fingerspelling, to fingerspell lists of words on videotape. A group of thirty-four experienced readers of fingerspelling, twenty-six of whom
were deaf people, viewed the tapes and transcribed the
words. Significant differences in intelligibility among the
ten senders were found, but the variation was not related to
being deaf or hearing or to length of experience.

People also vary in their ability to learn fingerspelling. A
study of problems in learning by hearing adults indicated
an age difference, and special difficulty in acquiring receptive skill (Savage et al., 1981). Twenty subjects, all connected with a school for deaf children, attended fingerspelling classes for ten weeks. They were then tested in reading
lists of fingerspelled words on videotape and in sending lists
of words themselves. Two significant findings emerged. The
younger subjects, up to age twenty-five years, were more successful in learning new fingerspelling skills than the older
subjects. Receptive ability was lower than expressive ability,
this being particularly the case for the older subjects.

IMPLICATIONS FOR EDUCATION   Although fingerspelling
is a manual representation of written language, it is used as
a substitute for speech as a live, or face-to-face, medium of
communication. In purpose, then, it is a manual means for
doing the work of spoken language.

Being *isomorphic* with written language, in that it has
word-for-word correspondence, fingerspelling can transmit
the correct syntax of English or other written language. Its

use might reinforce reading and writing skills. There have been reports of young Russian deaf children acquiring good vocabularies through early exposure to fingerspelling (Morkovin, 1960; Moores, 1972). Once learned as a system, or code, fingerspelling has infinite use within an individual's own limit of literacy. As such, it serves as a rapid and accurate means of instruction in school subjects. In comparison with speech and lipreading, fingerspelling has the special benefit that it facilitates communication between deaf children.

When the introduction of fingerspelling into an educational system is contemplated or a change is made in the form of manual alphabet used, questions arise as to how long it might take for older deaf children to learn fingerspelling, or if the transfer to a different form of fingerspelling will give rise to confusion. In a British study of problems involved in learning fingerspelling, older deaf children who were already experienced in using two-handed fingerspelling made rapid progress in acquiring ability to read one-handed fingerspelling (Savage et al., 1981). This suggests that the use of different forms of manual alphabets is a code-switching process, rather in the nature of reading upper- or lower-case forms of the graphic alphabet. The study also confirmed that when older deaf children had gained proficiency in fingerspelling, they achieved very high levels of accuracy for word recognition. Fingerspelling had a valuable place in their instruction as a "lexical tool" for learning new names or technical terms and learning the normal orthographic spelling at the same time.

A further British study with children learning fingerspelling (Dawson, 1976) looked at the effects of active assimilation on learning new words. The children were tested for learning of written and fingerspelled forms of new words presented under two conditions: with "active fingerspelling" of the words by the children, and with "passive" reception. It was found that the learning of the new words, both written and fingerspelled, was significantly better when the children fingerspelled to themselves at the same time as the words were presented, suggesting that the kinaesthetic feedback, or internalized feeling, from fingerspelling reinforced learning.

In *signing*, gestures and movements of the hands, known as *signs*, carry linguistic information much as words do in spoken language. This chapter considers some linguistic and psychological aspects of signing, with particular interest in those features which have relevance to the total communication approach to language development and to education.

It deals with signing in its own right as language but also in association with spoken (or written) language. For simplicity, these are explained in relation to English unless specifically indicated.

Signing will be described in three broad linguistic categories: sign language, as an independent language form; the blending of sign language and English, as Sign-English; and signed English systems for representing in manual form the syntax of English.

SIGN LANGUAGE   In *sign language*, manual gestures, together with bodily and facial cues, form *signs* which have meaning in themselves and are ordered according to their own syntactic rules. Sign language has been said to be the primary language used for communication among deaf people (Siple, 1978). Indeed, American Sign Language (also referred to as ASL or Sign) has been reported to be the fourth most common language in use in the United States (Mayberry, 1978). As there are many spoken languages, so there are many sign languages in use by deaf people in different countries. There are also regional and local variations in sign languages.

Spoken language and sign language differ in the way in which they are produced and perceived. In spoken language, words are articulated through voice by one person

American Sign Language   British Sign Language   Danish Sign Language

Figure 10. Signs for MOTHER in three sign languages

and normally received through hearing by another person. In sign language, signs are produced on the hands of the sender and received through vision by the receiver. Research into sign language and its use has been motivated largely by the questions, To what extent do spoken language and sign language have different properties which are dependent upon modality, and to what extent do they share properties which are independent of modality? With these questions in mind, some findings can be examined from research into the linguistic structure and psychological aspects of perception and acquisition of sign language.

The linguistic study of sign language had its foundation in the pioneering work of Dr. William Stokoe at Gallaudet College in the late 1950s. Since that time, linguists and psychologists have taken an increasing interest in American Sign Language. In the 1970s, research also developed into signing and sign languages in use in other countries, including Israel (Namir and Schlesinger, 1978), Sweden (Bergman, 1979), Denmark (Hansen, 1980) and Great Britain (Brennan and Hayhurst, 1980). The study of American Sign Language has provided information on its linguistic structure at levels corresponding broadly to the phonological, lexical, and syntactic levels of spoken language.

At the "phonological" level, signs are made up of parts which combine to give the meaning. This might be understood better by referring to the phonological elements of speech sounds. With the advent in the 1950s of what was termed transformational or generative grammar, a "generative phonology" approach was evolved to describe language. An important aspect of this approach was the use of *features*, the breaking down of speech sounds into their various parts. Ingram (1976) clearly explained this: for example, [p] is a *stop* sound, is *labial*, and is *unvoiced*; whereas [v] is a *fricative* sound, is *labiodental*, and is *voiced*. Stokoe (1960) discovered that the manual components of signs can be divided into parts. He first suggested that each sign has three features, or aspects, from which it can be described. These features or aspects are the *location* in space where the sign is made in relation to the signer, the hand *shape* (or hand shapes) used, and the *movement* involved in making the sign. Stokoe used the terms *tab*, *dez*, and *sig* for these aspects of the production of signs.

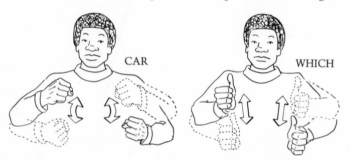

Figure 11. Two signs which are identical in location and movement, but differ in hand shape

Figure 12. Two signs which are identical in hand shape and movement, but differ in location

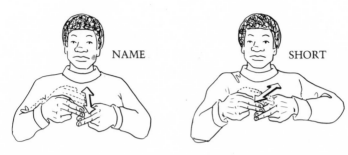

Figure 13. Two signs which are identical in location and hand shape, but differ in movement

Stokoe (1978) has identified a total of fifty-five such aspects—twelve of place, twenty-one of hand shape, and twenty-two of movement. These elements of signs, which Stokoe (1960) termed *cheremes*, correspond roughly to the sounds, or phonemes, of spoken words. Some of the hand shapes are similar to the formations of the American Manual Alphabet, and for this reason they can be described by the corresponding "letter" or "number," for example, [A-hand, 5-hand]. Some aspects, which look similar and do not act as distinctive features in the contrast of signs, were grouped together as *allochers*, corresponding to the allophones of spoken language, for example, [K-hand and P-hand]. Stokoe also designed a set of graphic symbols for recording the hand shapes, movements, and locations of signs in written form.

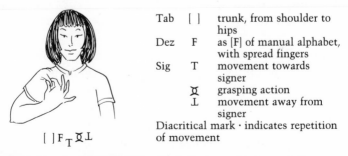

Tab	[ ]	trunk, from shoulder to hips
Dez	F	as [F] of manual alphabet, with spread fingers
Sig	T	movement towards signer
	⊠	grasping action
	L	movement away from signer

Diacritical mark · indicates repetition of movement

[ ]F_T⊠L

Figure 14. Sign for VOLUNTEER with Stokoe's graphic transcription

It has subsequently been pointed out that a fourth aspect, *orientation*, or spatial relationship of the hands to each other or to the body, is essential for a complete description (Battison, 1974; Friedman, 1975; Frishberg, 1975).

CHAIR

Figure 15. The sign for CHAIR, which differs minimally in orientation from the sign for NAME

As with speech sounds in spoken languages, the actual elements of signs might vary in different sign languages. It has been shown, for instance (Bergman, 1979), that the signs used in Sweden are made up of a larger number of elements than the signs of American Sign Language.

The research groups studying British Sign Language have cooperated closely in order to agree on a common notation system. They have worked together to modify Stokoe's transcription system and extended it to cover some additional hand shapes not found in American Sign Language and also to describe the orientation aspect. The resultant system for coding British Sign Language will help to ensure that the work of the British researchers will be mutually intelligible from the start (Brennan, Colville, and Lawson, 1980).

In addition to these aspects of the manual component of signs, attention has been drawn to the importance of facial expression, eyes, and whole bodily orientation in adding to the meaning of the sign (Baker and Padden, 1978). These might be thought of as the nonmanual component of signs.

The potential number of combinations of these elements is large, but it has been observed that formational con-

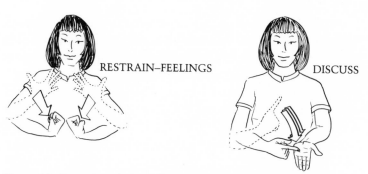

RESTRAIN–FEELINGS

DISCUSS

Figure 16. Examples of signs showing symmetry and dominance constraints

straints determine which combinations can occur as actual signs in American Sign Language. Two prominent constraints have been described by Battison (1978): (a) For two-handed signs, both hands have identical shapes and movements; this is the *symmetry* constraint. (b) The related *dominance* constraint determines that, if the two hand shapes are different, only one hand will move. Further, the passive hand is invariably one of a small number of hand shapes, viz., [A, S, C, G, B, 5 and O]. Battison (1978) suggests that these are the most natural basic hand shapes. Woodward (1978) states that the first six of these hand shapes "occur in most, if not all, the world's sign languages" (p. 341).

Signs tend to represent broad concepts, more so than the words of spoken language, and as such, they carry a heavier load of meaning. A point of concern to educators, and of relevance to the place of sign language in education, is the apparently limited size of the "lexicon" of signs in comparison with the wide vocabulary of spoken language. Cohen,

A   S   C   G   B   5   O

Figure 17. The basic hand shapes of American Sign Language

Namir, and Schlesinger (1977), in their dictionary of Israeli Sign Language, point out that "the vocabulary size of different sign languages has been variously estimated at anywhere between 1,000 and 4,000 signs" (p. 33). Certainly, the published dictionaries of sign language appear minute against the general dictionaries of spoken languages such as English.

The first extensive listing, based upon Stokoe's analysis of the parts of signs in *A Dictionary of American Sign Language on Linguistic Principles* (Stokoe, Casterline, and Croneberg, 1965), consisted of just in excess of 2,000 items. The Swedish National Association of the Deaf, for the revised and enlarged version of its *Sign Dictionary*, set a target of 2,600 signs (Bergman, 1979). *Sign-It*, the first authoritative dictionary undertaken by the British Deaf Association, was planned for 2,000 signs (Brennan and Hayhurst, 1980).

These dictionaries are not, in themselves, true reflections of the scope of sign language; but they do not claim to be exhaustive. Brennan and Hayhurst explained, for the British dictionary, "We do not suggest that this book will be a complete listing of all the possible signs in BSL . . . but it . . . will contain more information on the vocabulary of BSL than has ever been produced before" (p. 239).

Bellugi (1980), on the basis of extensive linguistic research, asserts that American Sign Language has a vast lexicon far richer than has been generally recognized. She gives reasons to believe that the vocabulary is richer than might be indicated by dictionary lists. Researchers are only beginning to describe the vast lexicon of signs in regular use by deaf people. It is also now understood that there are grammatical devices which expand the lexicon, corresponding to the process which in spoken language would be termed inflection or derivation. Detailed research in the 1970s revealed how signs can be modulated or changed in form to express different meaning by using space in a structured way (Klima and Bellugi, 1979).

In spoken language, grammatical change in meaning is commonly achieved through adding new words or by adding prefixes and suffixes, sound segments at the beginning or end of words. In sign language, the corresponding grammatical changes tend to be achieved through modifications in the timing, movement, and direction of signs. For example, the Danish sign for LOOK is made with a V-hand; changes in the direction of the movement change the meanings to LOOK UP, LOOK DOWN, LOOK TO THE RIGHT, LOOK TO THE LEFT, LOOK AROUND (Hansen, 1980).

Figure 18. Change of meaning by change of direction in Danish Sign Language

To take an example from American Sign Language, the sign for LOOK-AT has a variety of inflections for temporal aspect and focus to correspond with the English meanings *look at incessantly, look at continuously, look at regularly, look at for a long time,* and *look at over and over* (Bellugi, 1980).

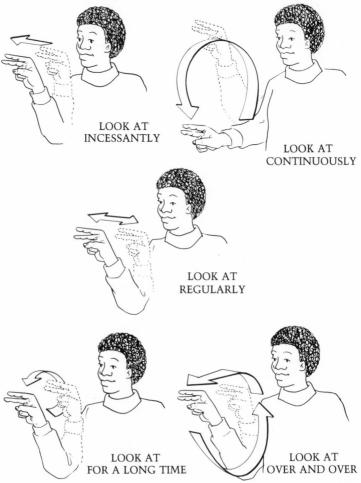

LOOK AT
INCESSANTLY

LOOK AT
CONTINUOUSLY

LOOK AT
REGULARLY

LOOK AT
FOR A LONG TIME

LOOK AT
OVER AND OVER

Figure 19. Change of meaning by change of movement in American Sign Language

Like spoken language, sign language continues to expand its vocabulary, or sign lexicon. Clear processes have been observed by which new signs are assimilated into American Sign Language (Frishberg, 1977). Signs are borrowed from other sign languages to fill existing gaps in the lexicon. Some signs, usually with grammatical functions, are also adopted from contrived signing systems (which will be described later). Another process, and one which is of interest to education, has become known as *initialization*; an existing sign for a broad concept is given more specific meanings corresponding to English words. This is done by changing the hand shape of the basic sign into the manual alphabet formations corresponding to the initial letters of the English words represented. For example, the sign for the concept CLASS is made with a [C-hand]; by changing the hand shape to the manual alphabet formation for the letter [G] the meaning of the sign is changed to GROUP. Making the sign with the [A-hand] represents the word AS-SOCIATION, and with the [T-hand] the word TEAM.

An example of both initialization and spatial direction used in combination is found in the signs for the compass points; the fingerspelling formations for [N, S, E, and W] are made with upward, downward, or sideward movements corresponding to their position on a map.

Initialization occurs quite naturally in American Sign Language as a good number of the hand shapes happen to be formations of the American one-handed manual alphabet. It is questionable whether the process would occur as naturally in British Sign Language using the British two-handed manual alphabet. A one-handed formation can be applied to a single-handed or a double-handed sign. But, a two-handed formation is not so readily applied to a double-handed sign, at least without violating the natural rule of two independently moved hands having identical shapes (and assuming that the symmetry constraint operates as fully in British Sign Language).

An explanation can be found quite readily in the different nature of the American and British manual alphabets. It has been seen that many formations of one-handed American fingerspelling also serve as the hand shapes of American Sign Language. The hand shapes of British Sign

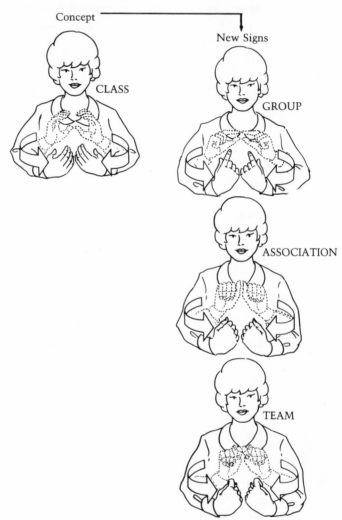

Figure 20. New signs formed by initialization of concept sign

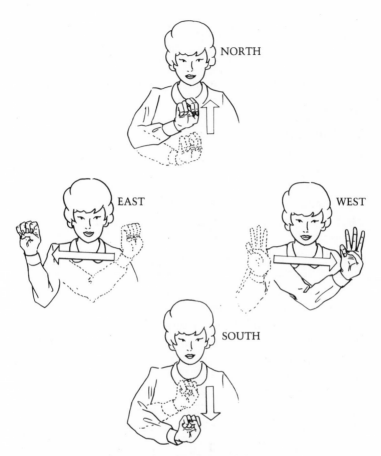

Figure 21. Initialization combined with spatial direction

Language do not come from the British Manual Alphabet but correspond largely to the formations of the American Manual Alphabet. (An examination of the formations of British Manual Alphabet shows that they are, in terms of Stokoe's analysis, two-handed "signs" which comply with the rules of symmetry, dominance, and basic hand shapes.)

Another indication of the natural assimilation of one-handed fingerspelling into American Sign Language is the number of fingerspelled words. Regular changes occur when words are fingerspelled as signs (Battison, 1974,

1978). For example, in words such as *job* and *back* the middle vowel letters are deleted and the fingerspelled signs are contracted to J-B or B-C-K.

Having outlined some features of the linguistic structure of sign language that might help in understanding the place of sign language in total communication, evidence of how sign language is perceived and how it is acquired by young deaf children will be considered.

One might expect the location and formation of signs to be determined largely by the movement of the body, arms, hands, and fingers of the signer. The general location of signs is the space in front of a circular area from the top of the head to just below the waistline. It has been suggested by Siple (1978) that the visual perceptual characteristics of the receiver might also determine the location of signs. She explains that, as visual acuity is best at the center of focus, finer discriminations can be made between signs at the point of focus than between those made farther away. As signers tend to look at the face for the nonmanual information, it should be expected that signs requiring finer discrimination of location and hand shape be made in this central area. In the outer areas of lower visual acuity should be found more two-handed signs which, being symmetrical, have added redundancy. Battison (1978) provided evidence that the seven passive hand shapes of nonsymmetrical signs occur significantly more frequently in signs made in the outer trunk area. In an experiment to test distinctive features, Lane, Boyes-Braem, and Bellugi (1976) found these hand shapes tended to be least confused in visual perception.

It takes longer to write something down on paper than it does to speak; it is possible, however, to read back at a faster rate than normal speech. The process of signing is somewhat analogous to this. Bornstein (1979) has drawn attention to two constraints, in production and perception, that have a bearing upon the rate of transmission of infor-

Figure 22. Areas for signing and fingerspelling (shaded)

mation in signing: (1) The body and manual dynamics of sign production appear to be slower than the mechanisms of vocal articulation. (2) Visual perception is less effective than auditory perception for temperal processing of linguistic information. Bellugi and Fischer (1972) have shown that in continuous discourse it takes almost twice as long to produce individual signs than it takes to articulate individual words, yet the rate of expression of linguistic meaning in sign propositions is about the same as in spoken sentences.

The explanation of this lies in the way in which sign language compresses complex meaning into signs through such devices as modulation of the movement, direction, and timing of the manual components of signs, together with the additional nonmanual information carried by the face, eyes, and bodily orientation. The spatial-grammatical features of sign language compensate for both the motor constraints of sign production and the visual constraints of sign perception. Grammatical information which is both produced and perceived in temporal sequence in spoken language is produced concurrently and perceived simultaneously in sign language.

Attention has been directed to the question of how signs are processed in memory. Experimental studies for spoken and written language have distinguished between two types of memory with different characteristics for organizing information. When hearing subjects are given short lists of words or letters to be recalled after a few seconds, the errors in recall tend to be items with similar sounding names, even when presented in written form (Conrad, 1970). This suggests that short-term memory is organized on the basis of sound, at a phonological level. But information in long-term memory, recalled after a longer period of time with the intervention of input of other information, is organized on a basis of meaning, at a semantic level.

Experiments on short-term memory for signs (Bellugi and Siple, 1974) show that, whereas hearing subjects are likely to have recall errors for words at the phonological level (for example, confusing *coat* for *coke*, which differ minimally by one sound), deaf subjects have recall errors for signs at the cherological level. The confusion is among similar aspects of the signs (for example, confusing NOON for TREE, both signs being made with one hand upright, elbow on palm of the nondominant hand, and differing minimally in aspect of hand shape).

In the study of long-term memory (Siple, Fischer, and Bellugi, 1977), lists of signs and written words were presented randomly to deaf students. After an interval, further lists were presented and the subjects asked to decide whether each item had been presented previously and whether in sign or word. The results suggested that both signs and words are organized in long-term memory on the basis of meaning. This is consistent with the way in which separate languages are treated by bilingual speakers.

This type of evidence leads to the conclusion that the short-term memory coding for signs, on the basis of aspect of place, hand shape, or movement, is modality specific; but long-term memory, being organized like memory for words on the basis of meaning, is independent of modality.

If long-term memory for signs is organized on meaning,

then it can be predicted that any special semantic characteristics of signs might influence the way in which they are
learned. One noteworthy feature of signs is known as *iconicity*. Some signs have a physical resemblance to the concepts or objects they represent. An object may be outlined
spatially (for example, BALL) but actions or states can also
be expressed pictorially (for example, SLEEP). Signs which
are iconic in origin tend, with usage, to change to more arbitrary forms (Frishberg, 1975), but some signs retain their
iconic identity, especially those that represent more concrete objects or concepts. Although iconic signs might be
processed by experienced adult signers in an arbitrary way
(Bellugi, Klima, and Siple, 1975), their pictoral representation would seem to be of importance to memory processing
and the learning of new signs by young children.

We can make two possible predictions: (1) Iconic signs
are more readily learned by young children than noniconic
signs. (2) The learning of such signs might be easier than
the normal learning of words. Brown (1977) carried out an
interesting experimental study that provided information
on these points. He required children to learn sets of new
signs, some of which had a physical resemblance to the objects represented, others with no pictoral clue to meaning.
Brown found that there was better learning of the iconic
signs than the noniconic signs. He further concluded that
the first signs might be more easily learned than the first
words of spoken language.

Linguistic studies of deaf children of deaf parents, exposed to American Sign Language in the home, have suggested some parallels between the acquisition of sign language and the normal acquisition of spoken language.
Hearing children begin vocal babbling from about six
months; in deaf children this takes the form of "gestural
babbling." It has been observed that young deaf children
can create their own spontaneous gestural system (Schlesinger and Meadow, 1972; Goldin-Meadow and Feldman,

1975). Hearing children begin to produce one-word utterances by the age of twelve months; it has been reported that deaf children can express similar meaning in one-sign utterances at this same stage (Skarakis and Prutting, 1977). There are reports of deaf children of deaf parents using one-sign utterances (Wilbur and Jones, 1974) and two sign utterances (McIntire, cited in Wilbur, 1976) earlier than the corresponding stages for spoken words. Using a method devised by Brown (1973) for observing the mean length of utterance of morphemes over time, Bellugi (cited in Siple, 1978) found that the deaf child acquiring sign language paralleled hearing children acquiring spoken language. Consistent findings of comparable three-sign utterances were reported in Dutch studies by de Jong-Koot and by Schermer and Gesmers (cited in Tervoort, Note 6). This type of evidence supports the contention that there are general linguistic universals underlying language acquisition which apply to sign language (Siple, 1978).

At the phonological level of language development, hearing children acquire certain speech sounds before others. Studies of the corresponding cherological development in young deaf children exposed to sign language (Boyes-Braem; McIntire, cited in Battison, 1978) suggest that the seven basic hand shapes already referred to, viz., [A, S, C, G, B, 5 and O], are among the first hand shapes to be learned.

SIGN-ENGLISH   It has been shown that sign language is not just a manual representation of spoken language. But signs might be used as a basis for representing the syntax of spoken language. The relationship between sign languages and signing of spoken languages is widely recognized (for instance, Bergman's study of Swedish Sign Language and Signed Swedish, 1979), but for simplicity of description, the following examples are of manual systems for signing in parallel to spoken English.

Sign language might be considered a natural language

form for deaf people in that its phonology, lexicon, and syntax are appropriately suited to the constraints of manual production and visual perception. The signs have meaning in themselves and are ordered in their own way, different from the words of English. But systems have been developed which are designed to represent the syntax of English. Woodward (1973) has suggested a sign continuum, with natural sign language at one end and the artificial sign systems at the other. In between is a mixture of sign language and English. This section will discuss this variety of signing, followed by a look at contrived systems which are more like codes for representing English.

Many deaf adults might be said to belong to a diglossic community; they use two main varieties of signing. With other deaf adults they can use, and might have a social and cultural preference for, sign language; but, in their contact with hearing people generally they are able to express themselves in the dominant language of English, using the signs of sign language as glosses for the words of English. Signs can be used, together with fingerspelling of some words, to approximate the word order of English. This, of course, presumes knowledge of English syntax. This variety of signing has evolved naturally out of sign language as a parallel to English. It has been likened to a "pidgin" form, or a mixture of the structures of both languages (Woodward, 1973; Bornstein, 1979).

Most hearing adults learning manual communication are likely to have difficulty with sign language structure and will adapt signs to English structure (O'Rourke, 1973; Bornstein, 1979). For communication between deaf and hearing persons, speech and lipreading are likely to become part of the process. (Some linguistic and perceptual aspects of the simultaneous use of oral and manual media will be discussed in the next chapter.)

Some difficulty is encountered over the use of different terms for this form of communication. As both the manual media of signing and fingerspelling are essential components, manual English is an appropriate description; this term has been applied, both in the United States (for example, at Washington State School for the Deaf, Note 14) and in Great Britain (Savage et al., 1981), but the term Signed English has also been used (O'Rourke, 1973). The situation is confounded further by the fact that the artificial systems, at the "contrived" end of the sign continuum proposed by Woodward, have been referred to under the generic term of Manual English (O'Rourke, 1973; Gustason and Woodward, 1973), although one of these systems is known as Signed English.

In dealing with these terms, it is important to be aware of exactly which system is referred to. In order to distinguish between the two forms of communication, this description will use the term *Sign-English* for the combination of signs and fingerspelling, on the grounds that they represent a mixture of "sign" from sign language and "English" from English language.

SIGNED ENGLISH SYSTEMS   Quite apart from the more natural use of the signs of sign language in conjunction with fingerspelling to approximate the syntax of English, just described as a Sign-English mixture, artificial systems have been developed to represent precisely the syntax of English. These will be described as contrived *signed English systems*, implying that they are signed representations of English syntax (without fingerspelling).

The idea of extending sign language by adding new signs, or devising an entirely artificial system goes back a long way. Abbe de l'Epée's system of methodical signs to parallel spoken French may be considered an early model. A system for signing the Dutch language was also in use during the early part of the nineteenth century.

A British system to represent the syntax of English was first conceived by Sir Richard Paget in the mid-1930s and was further developed by Dr. Pierre Gorman in the 1960s and 1970s into the *Paget-Gorman Sign System*. This is based upon the idea that each English word, or part of a word, should be given a sign and that these signs should be ordered and inflected in a manner corresponding to English. The system comprises basic signs for words of a common theme which are modified or accompanied by an identifying sign to provide more specific meaning. For example, the base sign for PERSON is made with one hand, and at the same time the specific sign to modify the meaning to DOCTOR is made with the other hand. Specific signs for affixes and auxiliaries are included in the system. The system has been tried in some schools for deaf children in England and Scotland and has been used in schools for hearing children with developmental language problems. In a linguistic study of the effects of the system with young children, Fenn (cited in Evans, 1978) considered that representation of words by basic signs in conjunction with the identifying signs actually "out-structures" English.

A number of contrived sign systems were developed in the United States during the 1970s. Three of these were historically connected—*Seeing Essential English* (Anthony, 1971), *Linguistics of Visual English* (Wampler, 1971), and *Signing Exact English* (Gustason et al., 1972). These three systems share a common aim of representing English in signs. In general, they invent new signs, modify existing signs, and create signs for affixes, word endings, plurality, and articles. They do not depend upon fingerspelling, although they might use the principle of initialization for closer sign-to-meaning correspondence. The differences rest mainly in the definition of the unit to be signed, the extent to which words are broken down, and the actual selection of specific signs. Of these three systems, it has been reported that Signing Exact English has achieved the widest use (Bornstein, 1979).

The other well-known contrived system is known as *Signed English* (Bornstein et al., 1975). This system comprises a lexicon of "sign words," corresponding in meaning to the words of English. As far as possible, the appropriate signs of American Sign Language are used. In addition, fourteen "sign markers" are used to represent common word form changes. These markers represent the regular and irregular plural and past, third person singular, -ing verb form, participle, adverbial, adjectival, possessive, comparative, superlative, agent, and prefix for opposite. For an example, the [D-hand] of American Sign Language indicates past tense, the [S-hand] indicates plurality. What cannot be represented by this system is added by fingerspelling the English words.

past regular verbs: walk*ed*

past irregular verbs: *saw*

ing verb form: speak*ing*

adverbs: ly quick*ly*

adjectives: y sleep*y*

Figure 23. The sign markers of Signed English

regular plural nouns:
bears

third person singular:
walks

plural irregular nouns:
[repeat the sign word twice]
children

possessive:
cat's

comparatives:
better

best

agent (person or thing):
teacher

Figure 23. (continued)

The preceding chapters dealt with the main media for visual reception of language. Having looked at speech and lipreading, fingerspelling, and signing—considering them as independent means of communication—attention will now be focused on the way in which these media, together with residual hearing, can be used in combination. Speech, being vocal, and signing or fingerspelling, being manual, can be produced at the same time. The concurrent use of both oral and manual media is known as *simultaneous communication*.

It could be presumed that reception through oral and manual media would provide additional information, or *redundancy*, with the possibility of parts missed in one medium being received in the other. But there could be some problems involved. Bonvillian and Nelson (1978) aptly point out that

such "redundancy" could only be helpful to the child who indeed was successfully processing considerable information in each of the modes—two channels of unprocessed information may constitute noise for the child rather than redundancy (p. 205).

This chapter is concerned with some linguistic and psychological aspects of the simultaneous use of oral and manual media. It considers the perceptual and cognitive processes involved and examines some findings from research into the effects on reception of linguistic information by deaf children.

COMMUNICATION AND INTERNALIZATION   The previous explanation of visual systems shows that descriptive terms have been used in different, even contradictory, ways (as, for instance, the interchangeable use of "signed English" and "manual English"). As a basis for clear and consistent discussion, a model of the simultaneous communication of oral and manual media will be offered. This might provide an understanding of the processes of production and perception and also define the way in which terms are used in our description.

With the help of Figure 24, the process of language communication in people with normal hearing is considered. Essentially, in communication through spoken language, one person expresses a message through speaking, and a second person receives the message through hearing. The *modality* of transmission can be described as *vocal-aural*, as the expressive medium is speaking and the receptive medium is hearing. The reception of the message by the second person leads to cognitive activity, such as memorizing, reasoning, or conceptualizing. As this activity uses words to represent objects and concepts, this can be termed *symbolization*.

In written language, expression is by writing, reception is by reading, and information is transmitted by a *motor-visual* modality. The words are transmitted in written form, but these can be understood as having the same meaning as corresponding spoken words. The process, in which different sensory images are translated into impulses compatible with past experience, is well described by Child (1977).

Consider how many ways you have experienced the concept "rose"—spoken word, written word, touch, smell, sight . . . but all have been transformed to a common code. So there is a wide latitude within which sensory experience is given a common meaning . . . the nervous system must carry out appreciable transformations of the input of physical images in order for perception to take place (p. 65).

In the example of written and spoken language the external graphic and acoustic signals are *decoded* into a form that allows cognitive processing. The product of cognitive activity might be new concepts which can be *encoded* into written or spoken form.

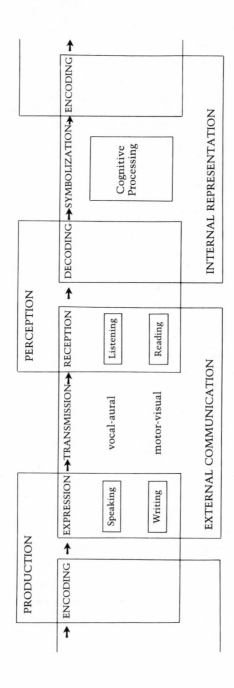

Figure 24. Communication and internalization of language

In this descriptive model it will be seen that *production* comprises both encoding and expression, and *perception* comprises both reception and decoding. Production by one person and perception by another is linked by *transmission* of information. Within an individual, *symbolization* takes place between perception and production. Thus, *external communication* includes expression, transmission, and reception; *internal representation* includes decoding, symbolization, and encoding.

This model can be developed to observe what changes occur in the simultaneous communication of oral and manual media. Figure 25 explains that the transmission is multimodal, but also complex. The two expressive media are speaking and production of signing in conjunction with fingerspelling; for convenience, these can be labeled signing/fingerspelling. The three receptive media are listening, lipreading, and reading of signing/fingerspelling. This poses some questions about perception.

For a person with sufficient residual hearing to benefit from a hearing aid, the reception of speech is both aural and visual; transmission is by a vocal-aural/visual modality. This requires the same linguistic information to be received simultaneously through hearing and lipreading. This problem has been the subject of a series of experimental studies which have shown consistently that the simultaneous use of lipreading with aided hearing gives better reception and understanding of speech, or *receptive intelligibility*, than either hearing or lipreading separately (Albright, 1944; Numbers and Hudgins, 1948; Hopkins, 1953; Prall, 1957; Hutton, 1959; Evans, 1960; Reeves, 1961; Duffy, 1967; Erber, 1971; Reich, Nickerson, Bick, Mierle, and Michal, 1976).

Hearing and lipreading involve two separate receptive modalities, aural and visual, but lipreading and signing/fingerspelling share visual reception. This raises the question, Can two separate visual signals be received simultaneously? In Britain, doubt about this possibility has been a

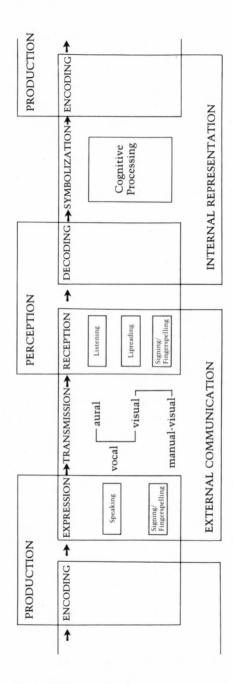

Figure 25. Simultaneous communication in oral and manual media

reason for excluding manual communication from educational practice. Watson (1976) claimed

it has not been shown that it is possible to perceive two visual media of communication. A deaf person watching a "combined utterance" may switch from one medium to another or rely entirely upon one, according to choice but evidence so far suggests that he is not getting information from both at the same time. On these grounds ... we would reject these methods as a supplement to oral methods for the development of language in schools for the deaf (p. 6).

Evidence for this view was not specified by Watson, but from a Canadian study, there was indirect evidence to suggest that deaf children can indeed receive information from oral and manual media at the same time. Reich and his colleagues (1976) presented prose passages to deaf children aged from nine to twelve years under various conditions. They found that the level of intelligibility for lipreading combined with fingerspelling was better than for either of these media on its own.

Some understanding of how fingerspelling combines with lipreading emerges from the work of Fisher and Husa (1973). They observed that fingerspelling formations vary in their intelligibility, but that some consonants which are difficult to distinguish on the lips are distinct in their corresponding handshapes. This allows fingerspelling to act as a partial cueing system to help resolve the ambiguities of lipreading.

For combined reception by lipreading and fingerspelling to take place, it is, of course, necessary for both the mouth and the hand of the sender to be within a suitable area of focus for visual perception. The study by Reich (1976) provided some information on the optimal hand location for reception of one-handed fingerspelling in conjunction with lipreading. Four different locations of the hand were compared (for right-handed senders): (a) six inches to the right of the mouth; (b) extended twenty-four inches to the right of the mouth; (c) in front of the right shoulder at a level eight inches below the mouth; and (d) at the waist eighteen inches below the mouth. Combined reception was best with the hand located six inches to the right of the mouth.

In simultaneous communication, signing also has a prominent role. The description of signing in the previous chapter explained that individual manual signs take longer to produce than spoken words. In sign language, this is compensated by the concurrent encoding of grammatical features, what we might think of as the "spatial compression" of meaning into a production rate comparable to spoken language. But in simultaneous communication, signs tend to represent words. Cokely (1980) has pointed out that when the signing is based upon one of the contrived systems, there is a particular problem of production rate. These systems use signs to represent English words but also use additional specific signs for syntactic features. Thus more signs might be required than spoken words to represent the same English sentence. It has been observed that, for this form of signing in conjunction with speech, there is a substantial amount of deletion and error (Baker, 1978; Marmor, Strauss, and Petitto, 1979).

A similar problem has been reported for fingerspelling at speed. Reich and Bick (1976) observed that teachers achieved a fingerspelling rate comparable with their speaking rate only at the expense of accuracy and completeness. It has been estimated by Bornstein (1979) that a comfortable rate for fingerspelling is 60 words a minute, or 40 percent of the average rate of speaking.

Baker and Cokely (cited in Cokely, 1979) observed what actually happens in simultaneous communication; they measured the production rates for manual signs and spoken words in combination. They found that hearing subjects decreased by 25 percent their normal speaking rate, to about 160 words a minute, and signed concurrently at a rate of about 90 signs a minute. Deaf subjects, using a form of Sign-English, had a higher rate of signing, about 100 signs a minute, but a lower rate of speaking, about 140 words a minute.

This information on fingerspelling and signing suggests that a comfortable production rate for simultaneous communication of English lies between 100 and 150 words a minute. This might be slower than normal speech, but, of course, the true choice for severely deaf people lies between a decreased rate of reception of English through simultaneous communication and a reduced level of intelligibility of normal speech through lipreading.

An intriguing question is whether the spatial aspects of signing have any implications in terms of what is known about cerebral specialization for language skills. The human brain has two parts, the cerebral hemispheres, which not only link with opposite sides of the body but have different functions in relation to cognitive skills. From the numerous findings of language disorders associated with left hemisphere damage, it has been inferred that for most (right-handed) people the left hemisphere is mainly responsible for the production and perception of spoken and written language.

Experimental studies have suggested that specialization for speech becomes established at an early age. Kimura (1963) presented groups of spoken digits simultaneously into both ears of normal children and determined lateralization by noting that digits heard in the right ear (and processed in the left hemisphere) were recalled better. Other researchers carried out similar experiments, using spoken syllables or words. Conrad (1979), in reviewing these studies, concluded, "There is now substantial agreement that cerebral dominance is established by about the age of four years and continues to develop for some years" (p. 255). Conrad also explained the findings of studies which show that different stages of reading development have different relationships with cerebral dominance: "earliest reading is predominantely spatial in character, while at a later stage more verbal elements associated with left-hemisphere dominance take precedence" (p. 255).

As long ago as 1876, it was proposed by Jackson (cited in Blanton and Brooks, 1978) that the right hemisphere has a critical function for visual recognition and visual memory. A series of early experimental studies (Weisenburg and McBride, 1935; Hebb, 1939; Brain, 1941; Paterson and Zangwill, 1944) found evidence of right hemispheric specialization for coding and interpreting spatial events. McFie (1972), from his study of the ability of brain-damaged people to write words and copy a geometric figure, concluded that there is lateral specialization in which the left hemisphere is related to verbal skills and the right hemisphere to spatial skills.

Findings from numerous studies enabled Neville (1976) to outline a broad pattern of cerebral specialization.

The left hemisphere analyzes over time, notes conceptual similarities, perceives detail, codes sensory input in terms of linguistic descriptions . . . whereas the right hemisphere synthesizes over space, notes visual similarities, perceives form, codes sensory input in terms of images (p. 198).

This leads to the consideration of how the visual images and spatial grammar of sign language are processed. There is scant evidence on the question of hemispheric specialization for signing, although some relevant information is available from an experimental study with hearing subjects (McKeever, Hoemann, Florian, and Van Deventer, 1976). Tachistoscopic (very short visual exposure) presentation of conflicting stimuli were made in the left and the right visual fields. The results of the study suggest that orthographic language stimuli—words and letters—tend to be processed in the left hemisphere, but manual language stimuli—signs and fingerspelling—tend to be processed in the right hemisphere.

Signing certainly involves processing of spatial information which normally includes right hemispheric activity.

How will this affect language perception and production? Coltheart (1980) has explained that (in hearing subjects with no brain damage) both concrete and abstract words can be processed in the left hemisphere, but abstract words are more difficult to process in the right hemisphere. Coltheart further referred to experimental studies of a condition termed *deep dyslexia* (which he defined as difficulty in reading and writing associated with left hemisphere damage) in which ability to read aloud depends upon the parts of speech represented by words. Subjects with this condition, who are therefore presumably using residual linguistic capacities of the right hemisphere, are able to read nouns best, followed by adjectives and verbs, but have difficulty in reading articles, prepositions, and conjunctions.

Given that spatial perception is specialized in the right hemisphere, if it is assumed there is a similar specialization for signed as for written and spoken words, it can be inferred that there will be facility for signing the *content* words of English which carry the semantic information, but perhaps less capacity for signing the *function* words which are essential for conveying the syntactic information. Previous discussions showed some possibly related evidence (Siple et al., 1977) that signs are stored in long-term memory on the basis of meaning at the semantic level, which might favor processing of signs for content words.

It is known that, in practice, signing can be used in conjunction with fingerspelling and lipreading to fully represent English. The research evidence allows a tentative explanation of the interaction of the linguistic, neurological, and psychological aspects of simultaneous communication. Signs can convey the semantic information of content words but do not represent the function words so well. The function words tend to be short (for example, *a, on, of, to*) and cannot be understood easily through lipreading, as word length affects visual perception of speech (Taaffe and

Wong, 1957; Erber, 1971). Lipreading involves much "guessing" among homophenous words to fill perceptual gaps from the context of whole sentences. It has been suggested by experimental study with hearing subjects (Treisman, cited in Herriot, 1970) that guessing of function words of spoken language is dependent upon semantic cues further away in the sentence. But long sentences are said to be more difficult to lipread (O'Neill, 1954; Clouser, 1976). The short function words can, however, be transmitted accurately by fingerspelling or by initialized signs. For example, the articles *a, an,* and *the* are made in simultaneous communication by fingerspelling [A] with sideward movement, [A-N], and [T] with a turn (Riekehof, 1978). These different media might therefore have complementary roles—signing to represent content words, and fingerspelling to convey the function words—which together synthesize into a form that closely represents, or has syntactic compatibility with, spoken or written English.

LINGUISTIC EFFECTS   There is evidence, from a number of studies, on the use of combined media with deaf children. In a study of American deaf adolescents, Klopping (1971) found that language reception was better when fingerspelling was added to lipreading and that the addition of signing led to a further increase. Similar results were obtained by Montgomery and Lines (Note 5) for Scottish deaf children. This incremental effect was confirmed in another British study of deaf children aged between eleven and sixteen years (Evans, 1978). For the particular type of language material used, in this case requiring discriminations of minimal differences in English syntax, fingerspelling contributed to a 50 percent increase in intelligibility over lipreading alone; with the addition of signing, there was a 40 percent increase over lipreading and fingerspelling combined. In a study by Grove, O'Sullivan, and Rodda (1979), which allowed deaf adolescents to use either pure oral or combined media according to their own personal preference, combined oral and manual media were found to be superior for transmitting various types of linguistic material. The researchers concluded that this superiority "extends into the most complex syntactical message classes" (p. 539). Taken together, the evidence of these studies offers confirmation of improved efficiency of simultaneous communication in oral and manual media.

Lipreading, fingerspelling, and signing have been described as the manual-visual means of transmitting language. These, together with residual hearing and lipreading, are the elements of simultaneous communication; with reading and writing, they comprise the main means for systematic transmission of English. Gesture, mime, and graphics further enhance communication, and sign language enriches social interaction and promotes cultural enjoyment.

The concept of total communication encompasses a wide network of activities, but spoken language, fingerspelling, signing, and written language constitute the linguistic core. Being capable of consistent transmission and internal symbolization of linguistic signals, these are the media of special relevance to linguistic and cognitive growth. The findings from research provide an understanding of the *structure* of total communication, the optimal combination of media for language communication; it is also necessary to understand the *strategy* for total communication, the optimal sequence of introduction of these media for language development. This chapter considers research findings that have some bearing upon the construction of a theoretical model for such a developmental strategy.

Since the concern is with visual language development as a substitute for the normal sequence, the source of reference can be the normal course of language growth. By the age of twelve years or so, a hearing child (with no significant learning problems) has well-developed language. To the extent that spoken and written language skills enable the child to think, to communicate with others, to learn at school, and also to use and interpret the array of communication media in the broader sense (film, television, art, drama, books), these constitute the core components of "total communication" for the hearing child.

The broad sequence in which these skills are acquired is known, of course, because it is a natural occurrence. This is represented in Figure 26. Original language competence is acquired first in spoken language. A receptive phase is followed by an expressive phase; language comprehension usually precedes production by a few months. The milestones of vocalization and speech development, as described by Lenneberg (1967), are relatively constant by age. By the age of four months, the child responds to speech sounds, turning the head and eyes as if to seek the speaker. By six months, earlier vowel-like sounds change to babbling, resembling one-syllable utterances. By twelve months, there is evidence of understanding some words and simple commands, and spoken words are emerging. At eighteen months, there is a small repertoire of words. By twenty-four months, there is a vocabulary of more than fifty items which can be joined into two-word phrases. At three years, there is a vocabulary of some 1,000 words, most of which are uttered intelligibly. By four years, language is basically established; the grammatical complexity of utterances is about that of colloquial adult language.

In general, spoken language emerges between two and three years. Up to the age of twelve years or so, the possibility for primary language acquisition continues to be good. After that time, the capacity for original language acquisition is lost; in terms of brain maturation

the ability for self-organization and adjustment to the physiological demands of verbal behavior quickly declines. The brain behaves as if it had become set in its ways and primary, basic language skills not acquired by that time, except for articulation, usually remain deficient for life (Lenneberg, p. 158).

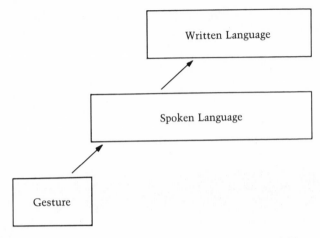

Figure 26. Developmental sequence for language in hearing children

From about four years of age, usually as the child begins formal education, written language is introduced. As written language is a secondary "code" for representing spoken language, reading and writing skills are learned as a transfer from competence in spoken language.

As expressive language emerges, words are associated with the objects and actions they represent. Presumably, earlier cognitive associations are built up with perceptions during the receptive stage. Piaget (1962) described a stage of cognitive development, which he termed sensorimotor, before the child is ready to deal with symbols that mark the beginning of language learning. At about the age of six months, the child sees a familiar object, such as a rattle or toy, and performs in a reduced form the action habitually associated with the object, which Piaget called "motor recognition." Brown (1973) suggested that the first sentences are built upon the earlier nonlinguistic process. "Where should the meanings of the first linguistic constructions come from if not from the sensory motor intelligence which directly precedes them?" (p. 199)

There is some interesting evidence to suggest that, in advance of the capacity to produce spoken words, gestural behavior is used with some ulterior purpose for future development. Bates, Camaioni, and Volterra (1975) observed in three infants the emergence, from the age of about nine months, of prelinguistic expression through gesture, pointing, and use of objects for pulling or as tools. They interpreted this gestural behavior as "protolanguage," which implies not only a substitute, but an actual preparation, for subsequent verbal behavior. In our model, this early gestural activity is shown as an overlapping, or transitional, phase between reception and the emergence of expression of spoken language. However, it has been suggested by Givens (1977) that, after verbal communication is established, this prelinguistic activity is not lost but is transformed into the gestural activity of adults.

COMMUNICATION SEQUENCING   It is appropriate now to consider the construction of a model of language development for deaf children (who, for the sake of this basic discussion, should be presumed to have no severe additional disabilities). If severe deafness can be defined as being of such degree and type of hearing loss as to prevent understanding of speech, such a condition from birth or soon after must, by virtue of the definition, preclude the possibility of acquiring spoken language through hearing. For children with such deafness, original language competence will have to be secured through a substitute medium.

The traditional oral philosophy has placed lipreading, as a vocal-visual biproduct of normal speech, in the substitute role for hearing. But the concept of total communication is founded on the view that lipreading, certainly lipreading alone, is an inappropriate medium for this purpose.

The pure oral approach was criticized by Lenneberg (1967) on grounds of the theoretical inadequacy of lipreading for language acquisition. He explained that contact with language is dramatically reduced in amount in comparison with the amount of language to which a hearing child is exposed, and that deaf children

> have to process visually what other children receive aurally. The latter point is of no small consequence because there are indications that the eye is slower in its temporal integration than the ear, and, therefore, even if perfection could be attained in lipreading ... ordinary discourse would be so fast that only small parts could be followed adequately (p. 321).

Vernon (1974) pointed out that prelingually deaf children taught by exclusive oral means "are expected to learn language through a process which presumes that they already have language skill" (p. 96). Conrad (1979) concluded from the results of his own research

> that lipreading does not provide prelingually deafened children with easy access into language. The inescapable problem of the lack of visible distinctiveness at the level of phoneme, syllable, or word, will not easily be overcome, and we must seriously doubt the wisdom of insisting that lip reading of English remain the vehicle for learning a mother-tongue (p. 203).

Evaluations of the results of oral education (reported in Chapter 1) have indicated the limitations of lipreading as a basis for language development, and studies of the perceptual parameters of lipreading (reviewed in Chapter 3) have explained why this is so. Because the visual pattern of speech is an incomplete version of the aural pattern, it does not represent the syntax of English. Lipreading cannot, therefore, substitute for hearing as a means of English language acquisition. In terms of our developmental model, formal attention to training of lipreading skill is reserved until a later stage of development.

Signing   There is evidence on sign language, both its acquisition and linguistic properties, that supports the early use of signing as a medium for gaining primary language competence. Mention was made (in Chapter 5) of studies of deaf children of deaf parents, exposed to American Sign

Language in the home, which have revealed some parallels between the acquisition of sign language and normal acquisition of spoken language.

An interesting study was made by Prinz and Prinz (1979) of the linguistic development of a child, with a deaf mother and a hearing father, who was exposed to both American Sign Language and spoken English from an early age. The first sign appeared at the age of seven months, but the first word appeared at age twelve months. Up to the age of twenty-one months the child produced on average 43 percent more signs than spoken words at given levels. It has been observed that young deaf children can create their own spontaneous gestural system, incorporating similar stages to hearing children learning spoken language (Schlesinger and Meadow, 1972; Goldin-Meadow and Feldman, 1975).

In a Swedish study of a group of young deaf children exposed to sign language, Ahlgren (cited in Evans, 1981) noted that the children were actually linguistically advanced for their age. She concluded that this was due partly to the use of signing, using visual language during a phase when visual stimulation is important to linguistic and cognitive development.

In the description of sign language (in Chapter 5), mention was made of the property known as iconicity, or external pictoral resemblance to the concept or object represented. It has been shown by Brown (1977) that this property does have a bearing upon the learning of signs. In an experimental study he required children to learn sets of new signs, some of which had a physical resemblance to their objects, but others of which had no such pictoral clue to meaning. He found that there was better learning of the iconic signs than the noniconic signs. He also observed that some iconic signs were particularly easily learned, and suggested that these fell into a special category, corresponding to words which represent, in cognitive terms, a *basic object level* of concept formation (for example, *chair* is a more basic exemplar of the class of seating objects than *sofa* or *stool*). Rosch (1973) had earlier observed that, in normal development of spoken language, objects at this basic level of conceptualization tended to be first named by hearing children.

In their study of the child acquiring both signs and spoken words, Prinz and Prinz (1979) noted that some of the first signs to appear closely resembled their referents (for example, BALL). It was further noted that the early signs, as well as the early words, tended to conform to the notion of the basic object level of conceptualization.

In terms of the cognitive aspects of development, Bruner (1964) described a phase which is characterized by organization of percepts and images (which he called an "iconic" mode). He also postulated an earlier phase, an "enactive" mode in which events and actions are represented by internalized motor response. We have already noted the observations of hearing children using gestures to express nonverbal intentions. It would seem reasonable to infer that, in the early phase of development, deaf children will be especially receptive to what we might think of as *enactive* type signs which have an internalized feeling of resemblance to the actions they represent (for example, DRINK). Some of the early signs observed by Prinz and Prinz (such as, ICE CREAM) could be considered to have such a proprioceptive, rather than just pictorial, connection with their actions.

In Piaget's sensorimotor period, vocal cries and manual gestures, which precede the use of arbitrary "signs" to communicate meaning, are said to be essential to subsequent phonological development—the ability to discriminate perceptions is a prerequisite for later identification of words. For deaf children, the early exposure to gestures might serve as preparation for use of manual signs at a symbolic level. It would seem reasonable to postulate that the gestural phase leading to spoken language in hearing children (described as protolanguage by Bates et al., 1975) could be exploited for deaf children as a "protosign" phase. Such a foundation of natural gestural activity could be extended to a systematic use of signs, which assume the symbolic function of words, as a medium for acquiring language competence.

The early use of signing has been strongly advocated by Freeman, Carbin, and Boese (1981) in their guide to parents of severely and profoundly deaf children. These authors, from their backgrounds in psychiatry, education, and sociology, maintained that

> the oral-only approach involves unnecessary and dangerous risks, because of its concentration on what the child cannot do. . . . A solid educational approach requires, instead, an emphasis upon what the deaf child *can* do . . . strengths as well as weaknesses. There is no way at present to predict which deaf children can be successful with an oral-only approach. Because sign languages have not been shown to affect negatively a child's chances of developing good speech, it seems vitally important to use signing as early as possible (p. 87).

Speech   The early exposure to signing does not mean that access to a speech and lipreading environment should be closed to the young child. Rather, positive attention should be given to both signing and speech. Tervoort (Note 6), the Dutch linguist, advocated the use of signing as early as the deaf child is ready but also maintained

> as soon as possible the simultaneous spoken word ought to be added . . . as far as early speech reading can be developed in a spontaneous way, it should obviously not be neglected, at least as long as matters are not turned upside down and speech reading becomes a goal in itself (p. 10).

If it is accepted that there is a place for both speech and signing with young deaf children—as a foundation for subsequent linguistic growth and also as an input for cognitive development—the question arises, Can signs and words be learned at the same time, or will processing of aural and visual systems lead to some sort of neurological confusion? Fortunately, there are some research findings to help with this problem. Volterra (1979) reported observations of young hearing children which suggest that emerging symbolic capacity is "modality-free." She observed that children first built up play vocabularies in both spoken words and manual signs. At the early stage, one "name," either a word or a sign, was sufficient for each different situation, and "double entries" of both the word and the sign were rare. This process could be compared with the way in which, in early bilingual acquisition, words are used in one or the other of two languages, rather than both (Volterra and Taeschner, 1978).

Reference has already been made to the study of linguistic development in sign language and spoken English in the young hearing child of a deaf mother and a hearing father (Prinz and Prinz, 1979). Apart from the earlier emergence of signs, the findings of the study were consistent with the process observed in bilingual hearing children. The child used two complementary vocabularies with only a small overlap of items that were both signed and spoken. It was concluded that the child encoded either a sign or a word for a concept; she developed one semantic system with separate lexical entries from both languages.

Tervoort (Note 6), commenting on the early use of both vocal and manual vocabularies by hearing children, explained that as children attain the capacity for spoken expression, the two vocabularies diverge. Hearing children do not progress to imitation of signs but develop a dominant verbal vocabulary. Volterra (1979) has explained that this happens, not because the vocal modality is superior, but because hearing children are not normally offered a continuing symbolic gestural system for communication. Indeed, she emphasized that in symbolic development, gestural activity is used spontaneously with no specific input from adults, as in the case with vocal activity. The transfer to vocal expression in hearing children could be viewed as a functional choice, determined by the normal access to language communication in the vocal-aural modality. How can a corresponding choice to match the preferred modality of hearing-impaired children be provided?

In his study of the linguistic and cognitive functioning of British deaf children, Conrad (1979) astutely pointed out that when deaf children have the benefit of both oral and manual media, they will grow up in an environment that is "quasi-oral" to a degree that will be directly reflected by the extent of hearing loss.

It should be obvious that we do not propose that when children are exposed to sign language, speech in their presence should cease; children will derive most linguistic benefit from the language with which the sensory capacities are most compatible (p. 284).

In a pure oral approach, the child who proves to have the necessary ability for language development through residual hearing benefits, but the child who proves not to have such aptitude and who might, therefore, be seen retrospectively to have needed early exposure to signing loses out irretrievably. Conrad explained the seriousness of this loss. "We may assume that the neurological hazards of delaying a sign language input are as grave as delaying other linguistic input. . . ." He also gave the rationale for including signing. "Since we see no circumstances which would justify excluding speech from language environment, insofar as there is error when deciding the kind of intervention which would be appropriate, it is of the fail-safe type" (p. 320).

If early exposure to both oral and manual media is provided, then two options are kept open. If the child shows potential for oral language, subsequent emphasis can be placed upon communication through residual hearing, lipreading, and speaking; and if the child shows lack of oral potential, positive emphasis can be directed to the continuation of manual communication in conjunction with oral media as appropriate.

The concurrent use of speech and signing in education raises the crucial question, How can these be integrated effectively in teaching methodology? Bornstein (1979) has suggested that, because the syntax of sign language is different from that of English, training in speech should be kept distinct from signing or treated later as a second language learning task. But, at the early stage, the concern is not so much with simultaneous communication in speech and signing as with laying down foundations for speech articulation. If attention to speech is not to be delayed, the teaching methodology must coordinate the development of signing with the preparation for speech.

The experimental program described by Brill and Fahey (1971) at the California School for the Deaf, Riverside, provided a valuable insight into the early use of signs and speech. The preschool children learned signs for 350 concepts within a year. At the same time, speech training was also emphasized. The number of words in understandable speech ranged from four to fifty in individual children. The number of words that could be recognized by the children through lipreading ranged from six to one hundred. Brill and Fahey concluded, "The sign language comes naturally, and it can be used as a very important foundation for building a good speaking vocabulary. . . . We found the use of signs was a help . . . in teaching children to speechread" (p. 19).

The observations of total communication practice in schools (reported in Chapter 2) revealed that speech is taught in close interaction with signing, including sign language. For example, at the Kendall Demonstration Elementary School, speech training is based upon the scheme developed by Dr. Daniel Ling (1976) at McGill University. Ling's approach is modeled on the natural process in hearing children; detailed systematic training is first given in articulation of speech sounds—in the many combinations and with different pitch, intensity, and rhythm—before using in spoken words. Signing is used as a means for the actual explanation in teaching of this process; speech training is based upon prior and fuller competence in signing. Such a technique is consistent with the total communication approach, but, in fact, oral teaching has made use of manual means of explanation. The speech training method advocated in the 1960s by Sir Alexander Ewing at the University of Manchester linked the articulation of speech sounds to such referential concepts as "flick" of the tongue, "at the back" or "at the front" of the mouth. But in this method, these concepts, not being readily acquired through oral explanation to children without developed language competence, were actually taught by analogy to manual "signs" to represent the articulatory movements (Ewing and Ewing, 1964, p. 223).

Fingerspelling In the normal development of hearing children, written language is learned after spoken language has been established. In the case of profoundly deaf children, written language will be introduced after some original language competence has been acquired in signing or in signing and speech. But that is not all; if fingerspelling is to be used effectively, it also needs to be developed as early as possible. Should fingerspelling be taught as a tertiary code after the child has gained some competence in reading, or should there be mutual exposure to both fingerspelling and reading? There are some grounds for supporting the view that these two media should be used concurrently, or even that exposure to fingerspelling should precede formal introduction to reading.

A good proportion of the formations of the American, or International, Manual Alphabet are also handshapes of American Sign Language (but also of some other sign languages, such as British Sign Language and Swedish Sign Language). The earliest handshapes acquired in American Sign Language are also fingerspelling formations, viz., [A, S,

C, B, O, and G]. According to Woodward (1978), these handshapes occur widely in other sign languages. They are also common as fingerspelling formations in one-handed manual alphabets. The young child learning sign language will, as a matter of course, be using at least some finger-spelling formations, and this process might contribute to readiness for more formal fingerspelling production. Unlike graphic reading, fingerspelling is a "live" medium with, therefore, greater potential for early interaction with other language acquisition media.

There is a case for early use of sign language, or at least a sign language lexicon, for promoting internal language competence on grounds of visual qualities of iconicity and spatial grammar. But, if English (or the corresponding dominant language of the culture) is to be a target language for social and educational use, we must consider the problem of transferring from sign language to English. The contrived systems for signing English (mentioned in Chapter 5) are relevant to this problem. The three main American systems—Signing Exact English, Signed English, and Seeing Essential English—have all been used substantially in total communication programs, including the preschool level (Jordan et al., 1979).

Fingerspelling might contribute to the transfer to English syntax particularly in the representation of function words. We have discussed the capacity of signs to convey the content words of spoken language which carry the semantic information. It might be relatively easy for the young deaf child to build up an early lexicon of signs corresponding to content words. The observations by Brill and Fahey (1971) of the early signing of preschool children was consistent with this notion. Within the first year of introduction, the children learned a lexicon of signs which comprised, in terms of corresponding English words, 276 nouns, 35 verbs, and 32 adjectives, but only 5 prepositions and 6 question forms (p. 18).

As far as normal learning of language is concerned, when the basic skill of "naming" has been learned at an early stage, new words can be acquired indefinitely (Gleason, 1961; Lenneberg, 1967). But Cokely (1979) has explained that the most crucial need for the deaf child is for acquisition of syntactic competence; and it is believed that there is a critical period for acquiring syntactic competence in spoken language (Lenneberg, 1967; Chomsky, 1969; Brown, 1973). Assuming that similar urgency exists for acquiring manual representation of English syntax, there is the need to gain competence in the function words which are important for the syntactic structure.

In learning spoken language, hearing children tend to first use those function words that have the highest frequency of occurrence (Brown, 1973). But, of course, these words normally occur spontaneously in the aural environment. When planning a corresponding visual environment for the deaf child, which includes function words to complement the signed content words, we need to specify the appropriate vocabulary. Fortunately, relevant information has long been available. Dewey (1923) made an extensive study of the frequency of occurrence of words as represented in a wide range of materials—American newspapers and magazines, advertisements, speeches, fiction, personal and business correspondence, and scientific papers. Dewey was able to estimate the average frequency of the words encountered in the extensive sample. He found that, whereas such familiar words as *winter* and *tomorrow* occurred only once in 10,000 words, the twenty most frequently occurring words accounted for more than one third of all words. The ten most common words alone accounted for 27 percent of the total, and these were all functions words (viz., *the, of, and, to, a, in, that, it, is, I*).

Competence in using these words is normally gained early, before a child learns to read. Fingerspelling, being a live medium, might be suitable for representing function words for the deaf child at an early age. Possibly these short words can be learned as "signs" without regard to their spelling as such. Learning of the orthographic form of these words could well follow from fingerspelling, rather than the reverse process of learning fingerspelling from the written words. Teachers at the Maryland School for the Deaf and the Virginia School at Hampton confirm that young children can learn fingerspelled "signs" in this way, based directly on meaning, and later learn the written form of the words (Evans, Note 12).

Reading and Writing   In practice, it is likely that written language will be introduced early, and we can expect a close interaction between fingerspelling and reading in the transition from initial competence in signing to performance in English. Any planning of an early fingerspelling lexicon of function words would need to be coordinated with the reading vocabulary. An example of a British reading scheme compatible with the requirements for the fingerspelling lexicon has been used in conjunction with early fingerspelling at Northern Counties School for the Deaf. This scheme, based upon the concept of "key words" (McNally, 1965), starts off with just a small number of the most frequently occurring words of English. The early stages of the scheme use only 300 key words which (taking 20,000 words as an average vocabulary) make up three quarters of the commonly used words. The twelve most common key words represent one quarter of the entire normal vocabulary. All ten of the most frequently occurring words from Dewey's list are found in the basic twelve key words of this reading scheme.

The concern, here, is with earlier introduction to written language than is usually the case with hearing children. Lenneberg (1967), after examining the evidence on the written language of deaf children, strongly supported the early exposure of deaf children to graphically presented language material. He also advocated the acceptance by teachers of "primitive language productions and grammatical deviations" and the exclusion of "grammatical meta-language until a basic proficiency in language is fully established" (p. 324). Lenneberg meant, by this, the encouragement of spontaneous expression in advance of grammatical perfection, and the discouragement of any formal emphasis upon the grammar of a developing language.

Cokely (1980), in his analysis of the question of lexical and syntactic development in Sign-English, came to a consistent conclusion. He suggested that linguistically it would be a "sound approach to deal only with those elements of English syntax which are essential to the functioning of the language and to retain a semantically based approach to lexicon with a careful and guided addition of needed signs" (p. 28).

Reimer (1979), in a paper concerned very much with practical details in providing language development for deaf children (through the use of a signed English system), pointed out that hearing children, although exposed to a refined English pattern constantly, respond initially in a gross way which then gradually becomes more refined. She argued that "young deaf children should not be forced to speak/sign in complete sentences when young hearing children do not. We should keep our language demands of hearing-impaired more attuned to normal hearing children's language development" (p. 845).

At the early stage of development, it might be as well to accept a form of Sign-English which has a minimal basis of syntactic compatibility with English, but in due course, it will be important to progress to more exact syntactic representation of English in written form. Fingerspelling has a special potential in this transitional process. Being a live medium, it can interact with signing; having reversibility with orthographic spelling, it can represent written language. Content words originally learned as signs might gradually be relearned in fingerspelled form, and this might reinforce the subsequent learning of the written language.

With growth of written language, an influence can be expected to operate in the reverse direction. Through the process of initialization (explained in Chapter 5) by which change of handshape of a sign to correspond to the initial letter of an English word gives more specific meaning to a concept sign, there will be feedback from written language into signing.

Lipreading   The research evidence suggests that formal reliance upon lipreading, as a medium for language communication, may be delayed until there is growth of basic competence in English. It has been concluded in several studies that lipreading ability is dependent upon the level of existing linguistic knowledge (Pauls, 1960; Craig, 1964; Myklebust, 1964; Evans, 1965; Berger, 1972).

It has been demonstrated that in normal aural perception, reduced information of spoken language can be recognized through anticipation of the linguistic sequence (Shannon, 1948; Denes and Pinson, 1963; Fry, 1964). Presumably, in lipreading it is possible to use contextual knowledge of language in much the same way. An analogy can be made with the normal development of (graphic) reading ability. Smith (1978), in his analysis of the reading process, maintained that reading success depends not so much on what is seen on the printed page as on what is brought to it by the brain. He explained that

knowledge of the relevant language is part of information that is essential for reading, but it is not information that you can expect to find on the printed page (rather it is information you must have already) (p. 5).

From the evidence on visual perception of speech, it would seem reasonable to postulate that lipreading success is determined, not so much by what is seen on the lips, as by the linguistic knowledge that is brought to the task.

Knowledge of English, acquired through signing, fingerspelling, and reading and writing, will create a better condi-

tion for lipreading—the use of linguistic context to complete the visual perception of the speech pattern. It has
been emphasized that this approach need not deny the
child access to a speech and lipreading environment, concurrently with the encouragement of signing and fingerspelling. If the child proves to have capacity to benefit from
this informal exposure, then lipreading training becomes,
not the introduction of a completely new skill, but the positive reinforcement of an existing tenuous system.

BILINGUAL OPTION   Assuming that the deaf child can acquire skills in signing, fingerspelling, speech, and written
English, these media comprise the linguistic core of total
communication, at least as far as English language is concerned. However, the concept of total communication is
broader, gives a prominent place to sign language, and at-
taches much importance to its social and cultural use by
deaf people. But the use of sign language presupposes its
prior acquisition. From the report (Falberg, 1964) of the previous general absence of teaching of sign language in
schools for deaf children, we can infer that many American
deaf adults have gained knowledge of sign language independently of, or even despite, the formal educational oppor-
tunities at school. If the total communication philosophy
advocates an eventual choice for deaf people (to use sign
language, Sign-English, or both), then its methodology
must provide scope for an option.

It has been suggested that signing of English might be developed with the aid of fingerspelling, from the systematic
extension of the early gestural phase, through a lexicon of
sign language signs, into the temporal syntax of English.
From this same source, the development of sign language
will require, not so much a transfer, but a direct continuation of the early sign language lexicon into the spatial syntax of sign language. When the need to keep an option open
for speech development was discussed, a multimodal situation was being talked about—oral and manual media of En-

glish. When considering an option for sign language development, a bilingual situation is, in effect, being talked
about—English and sign language.

For the profoundly deaf child whose preferred modality
proves to be visual and who does not have early access to
aurally coded language, the medium for original language
competence will be signing. If there is early exposure to
formal sign language, it might be expected to establish itself as the natural first language of the child. In this case,
the later transfer will be to English as a second language.
The problem of delayed language learning has been emphasized, in particular the irretrievable loss of capacity for language acquisition beyond the crucial maturational stage.
But, of course, if it is accepted that sign language does meet
the basic criteria of language—capacity for consistent ex-

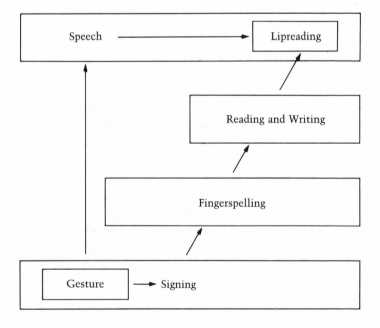

Figure 27. Developmental sequence for language in deaf children

ternal communication and internal symbolization—it might be assumed that it will serve to lay down the necessary neurological organization for subsequent language learning. As Lenneberg (1967) explained, when such cerebral organization has taken place, second language learning can occur into maturity.

DEVELOPMENTAL MODEL   It is now appropriate to bring together these ideas on the introduction and phasing of the different oral and manual media. The interpretation of the research findings, in relation to the aims of the total communication philosophy, leads to a model of a language development for deaf children the broad constructs of which are represented in Figure 27.

This might help the theoretical understanding of the optimal developmental sequence for different communication media, but there remains the considerable challenge of applying such a strategy in actual teaching methodology. This will be considered in the final chapter.

Evidence has been reviewed to suggest that, for people with severe deafness which precludes understanding speech through hearing alone, the optimal combination of media for communicating language will be drawn, according to individual needs and changing situations, from amplified hearing with lipreading, fingerspelling, signing, and written English; sign language; and Sign-English or a form of signed English. This has been described as the structure of total communication.

It was also argued that before a child can use these media for communicating language, it is necessary to first acquire competence in the different media. The theoretical model of the optimal sequencing for development of these linguistic media was thought of as the strategy of total communication. The implementation of theory in practice is now considered. The ideas of the previous chapter will be summarized in a form of action for teaching methodology, and then the practical implications will be discussed.

TEACHING METHODOLOGY The recommendations that emerge from the interpretation of research findings, linked with observations in schools, can be summarized as follows:

1. There should be earliest possible exposure to signing to assist in the acquisition of internal language competence and to promote cognitive development. The phase of natural gesture should be reinforced with a basic sign lexicon which emphasizes enactive type gestures and iconic signs. This phase should be extended into fuller use of symbolic signs and spatial syntax, as a foundation for sign language development. Concurrently, there should be exposure to speech by support of residual hearing and through visual re-

ception, both as a positive prerequisite to future simultaneous communication and as an option in the event that the child proves to have adequate aptitude for good oral communication. Early preparation for speech articulation might draw upon knowledge of signing as a medium for instruction in speech training.

2. A transfer of emphasis toward the target language of English would involve the use of signs to represent English words. This process might be promoted through close interaction of signs for content words and fingerspelled "signs" for an initial vocabulary of function words prior to a more complete system of Sign-English. Observations in schools suggested that this stage can be reached by the age of three years.

3. A fuller use of fingerspelling should facilitate the transfer to more complete representation of English syntax. This should proceed in close conjunction with the learning of reading and writing. From knowledge of written language and fingerspelling there should be feedback, through the process of initialization, to closer lexical representation of English in signing.

4. Increased competence in English should establish a more viable base for lipreading through the use of contextual cues.

In total communication philosophy, there is a sensitive appreciation of individual needs, a concern to offer the most appropriate medium, or media, according to different aptitudes and abilities. The preceding scheme is, therefore, a broad description of a flexible developmental sequence rather than a rigid prescription as to exactly how it should be used with all children. But children with profound hearing loss from birth who need to progress along such a path will encounter a range of language forms more complex than in normal development by hearing children: natural gesture, with the possible development of fluency in sign language; a form of manual English, or Sign-English, using signing and fingerspelling; and English, through simultaneous communication in speech and lipreading, fingerspelling and signing, or through reading and writing, or through a signed English system. When we consider the implementation of total communication, we need to take account of the ideas on the optimal combination of language forms and the optimal sequence for their development—the structure and strategy of total communication. This is represented in Figure 28.

PRACTICAL IMPLICATIONS   The extent to which this approach might be successfully applied, for individual children or in different schools and for subsequent social and educational use, will be determined largely by practical constraints. To put our theoretical ideas into practical perspective, we must consider the crucial problems which

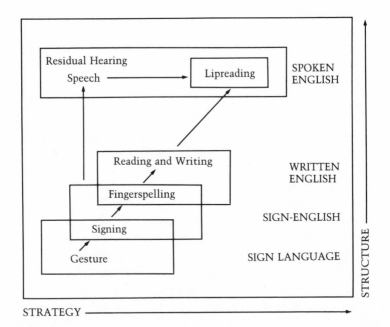

Figure 28. Total communication: Structure and strategy

arise, together with their implications for parents, teachers, administrators, and deaf people.

Additionally Handicapped Children   The basic discussion of language development has been centered upon severely deaf children with no signficant additional handicaps. But Freeman (1981) has reported that studies indicate between 20 and 40 percent of hearing-impaired children have additional disabilities. In particular, about one-third of children born with deafness due to maternal rubella have concomitant visual problems, and one survey showed a third of all deaf children have significant impairment of vision (Pollard and Neumaier, 1974). Additional handicaps, whether physical, sensory, or intellectual, can adversely affect the communication process. For instance, motor impairment due to cerebral palsy might hinder the production of signs, and particularly the finer movements of fingerspelling. Severe visual impairment might preclude any useful understanding of speech through lipreading and make reception of fingerspelling and signing difficult. Such conditions, being of their very nature complex, do not allow simple generalizations, other than to recognize that the selection and emphasis of different media will depend on individual response.

With some conditions, modification or substitution of the communication techniques will be indicated. This might be the case, for example, with Usher's Syndrome, congenital deafness accompanied by progressive impairment of vision. Hicks and Hicks (1981) have set out some practical suggestions for such children and young people in the total communication context.

For those students who still have good central acuity but a greatly restricted visual field, it may be necessary to substantially modify normal sign language procedures. Keeping in mind the three major components of sign language—point of location, movement, and configuration—it may be necessary to reduce the magnitude of the movements, increase the duration of each sign, and make each signed configuration clearer and more concise. As the field of vision becomes more restricted and as central vision deteriorates, other communication methods will have to be considered (e.g., ... touch method—alphabet in palm of hand, ... braille, manipulative alphabet) (p. 428).

An interesting technique has been used with a group of deaf children who are also autistic at St. Mary's School for the Deaf, Buffalo, New York (Young, Note 15). These children appear to perceive signs with understanding but have difficulty in producing signs themselves (a situation somewhat comparable to hearing autistic children who cannot express themselves in speech). It has been observed that the children gain satisfaction when the teachers manipulate the signs, molding the child's hands into the shapes and movements or actually making signs on the child's body (for example, the sign for PEACH made on the child's face). This seems to simulate for them the expressive activity of signing, perhaps enabling the child to experience the effect of "internalizing" the signs. From these observations we might infer that these children are able to encode concepts as signs, the locus of the difficulty being at the expressive level.

In the total communication approach, there is the possibility of finding the media or modifications that best correspond to the individual child's residual strengths. Observations in schools certainly confirm that total communication is relevent to the needs of additionally handicapped children. It is significant that in the experimental study of combined oral and manual communication reported by Brill and Fahey (1971), most of the preschool children in the program were deaf from maternal rubella. The experience of a British study is also noteworthy. When one-handed fingerspelling was introduced into a school curriculum, it was decided at the initial stage to exclude two classes of children with severe additional handicaps. However, although they were not taught formally in the classroom, "it was observed that the children were soon using fingerspelling proficiently to communicate with other pupils out of the classroom" (Savage et al., 1981, p. 168).

Higher Education   The need for total communication is likely to increase, rather than diminish, at the stage of higher and further education. Deaf students who have maintained progress at school because of combined teaching methods will probably continue to need access to both oral and manual media of instruction at college or university. It is also possible that of those deaf students who have made good progress through oral means because of the teaching, resources, and curriculum of a special school, some might choose the additional support of simultaneous communication in the more open environment at higher education level.

The United States is well endowed with postsecondary programs for deaf students. By 1980, there were two federally established national programs, Gallaudet College and National Technical Institute for the Deaf at Rochester Institute of Technology; four federally established regional programs; and at least a further thirty-five postsecondary programs, as well as four graduate programs for deaf students (Rawlings, Trybus, and Biser, 1981). In general, these colleges or programs provide special services which include instruction through both oral and manual communication, either by direct use of simultaneous communication by the teachers or through interpreters.

Special services have been developed in other countries. There are five programs in Canadian colleges. In Britain, support services have been set up in a number of colleges of further education and at the University of Durham. In Denmark, there is the National School for Continuing Education. In terms of total communication support, the essential requirements for developing programs include special classes (with direct teaching through simultaneous communication), interpreting services, and training in manual communication for the staff (and also for those deaf students who come from oral schools).

Parents   It is one thing to advocate very early exposure to signing; it is quite another proposition to expect all parents of young deaf children to sign fluently. There are studies which suggest linguistic benefits for deaf children brought up by deaf parents using sign language. But such children are a minority. In the United States approximately 90 percent of hearing-impaired children are born to parents whose native competence is in spoken language (Rawlings, 1973). Knight (1979) has pointed out that for sign language to assume anything approaching the level of native competence in the home environment, "the parents and other family members would not only have to learn a new language, but do so in an extremely short period of time. . . . It is doubtful whether this would ever occur to any significant degree" (p. 10). He considered, however, that it is not so much just formal sign language that must be used, but a language form that allows adequate communication between parent and child.

Freeman et al. (1981) also recognized that parents cannot usually learn formal sign language quickly enough to use with their own child at the crucial stage. For this reason, they accept that a form of signing approximating English is more likely to be mastered. But even the learning of a signed English system presents difficulties. Bornstein (1979) stressed that *"a sign system must be learned by members of the family during the very time it is used with a child in the home"* (p. 156), but that this is no easy task. He pointed out that learning Signed English, the simplest of the contrived systems, requires an immense investment of time and energy by a family. He recorded that in the parent guidance program of one school using total communication, after six months of weekly home visits, about 50 percent of mothers could use simple sentences in signed English and another 40 percent could sign words, but only about half of the fathers could sign.

At the earliest stage, full competence in signing might not be essential. At the outset, the child's exposure might be to a small lexicon of signs that come from sign language. If there is close coordination between work at school and guidance to parents, it could well be possible for parents to keep reasonably abreast of this developing lexicon and the early syntactic processes.

The experimental work described by Brill and Fahey (1971) at the California School for the Deaf followed such an approach. The mothers of preschool children exposed to signing with speech and fingerspelling were asked to attend one class session weekly with their children. The mothers were introduced to the new signs learned by their children, so that they could use the signs in the weekly class session at school. As the children were learning between ten and twenty new signs weekly, it was a reasonable expectation that parents might keep up with the expanding lexicon.

Teachers   When hearing parents have a deaf child, usually they have no previous knowledge of manual communication. Teachers of deaf children, on the other hand, might be expected to come to their work already proficient in signing and fingerspelling. It is especially crucial that teachers of young deaf children, who need to be conversant with both sign language and Sign-English or signed English systems, should be thoroughly prepared. This calls for adequate training in manual communication, both theoretical understanding and practical instruction, as part of the professional education of teachers of deaf children.

In some countries where total communication has been introduced into schools, some study of communication has been included in teacher training courses, but full practical instruction in manual communication skills might be missing. A very real problem is the way in which courses have been organized. In Britain, for instance, the traditional pattern has been for students to complete an undergraduate degree course in an academic subject, followed by a postgraduate course in education. Then, usually after a period of teaching in ordinary schools, the students enter a further specialized one-year course in education of deaf children. Such short courses do not allow an adequate span of time for acquiring competence—especially receptive skills—in manual communication, particularly for the more mature students. A case could be made for an integrated scheme in which undergraduate academic study would be followed by postgraduate professional training, but with instruction in manual communication offered concurrently throughout the whole period of study.

Changes in teacher training courses could influence the long-term development of communication skills of teachers, but in some countries the more immediate concern is for in-service training of teachers already in the schools. Fortunately, there is documentation of some experiences of schools which have undertaken such in-service training (Savage et al., 1981, pp. 158–166). In 1971, the Pennsylvania School for the Deaf at Philadelphia carried out a special program for the training of teaching and residential staff in close collaboration with Gallaudet College. Successive groups of staff from different departments of the school spent periods of intensive study at Washington, D.C., with follow-up instruction at the school. Within a year, the staff as a whole had gained reasonable working competence in manual communication skills. At about the same time, the Carver School in Maryland had made a similar change, from oral teaching to total communication, and the staff underwent a training program. Within a year, the staff and children had become proficient in signing and fingerspelling. These schools had, of course, the benefit of the wide knowledge and provision for manual communication training which has developed on an extensive scale within the United States. Such resources are not so widely available everywhere. A British school, changing from the mainly oral to combined teaching approach, found it necessary to send staff to the United States to gain working insight into manual communication training prior to setting up an intensive scheme. Fortunately, there has been much positive action toward provision of communication skills training for the general public which should be of great support for teachers and parents.

In Denmark, the Center for Total Communication at Copenhagen has made a significant contribution to in-service training. Instruction is available in Danish Sign Language and in signed Danish for teachers and parents (Hansen, 1980).

The growth of total communication in educational practice will strengthen the position of deaf people in professional roles in the schools. "It propels individuals who are skilled in manual communication into prominence" (Bornstein, 1979, p. 164). Deaf students might come to teacher training already skilled in manual communication, but they also have a special responsibility to the concept of total communication. As hearing teachers need to become proficient in signing, so deaf teachers need to be competent in English.

Not only deaf students, but also younger hearing students with aptitude for language learning, will have a special contribution to make. Bornstein pointed out the very real problem that

conversely, older individuals and persons skilled with other techniques are apt to become uncertain ... and acutely aware of their own limitations in manual communication. Needless to say, middle-age ... administrators will find it difficult to become truly fluent signers. Hence they are not likely to be as effective in monitoring this kind of change as they might be with more conventional techniques (p. 164).

Professional Cooperation The challenge is to ensure that change is effected through existing as well as developing expertise. Plans might be developed for a situation in which oral and manual communication skills are the conventional techniques of all teachers of all children, but the realization of this aim will require the support of education administrators with differing backgrounds. Such is the complexity of the whole problem of language development in deaf children, that its understanding draws upon various disciplines—audiology, speech science, psychology, linguistics—in addition to education. Progress for the deaf child will require cooperation between different professionals—some competent in theory, others proficient in practice; some deaf, others hearing; some skilled in manual communication, others not. The advance of total communication, as a liberal philosophy, will best be implemented through such an eclectic approach.

FURTHER READING

Educational Principles:
Moores, D.F. *Educating the Deaf: Psychology, Principles, and Practices.* Boston: Houghton Mifflin Company, 1978.

Communication Methods:
Henderson, P. (Ed.). *Methods of Communication Currently Used in the Education of Deaf Children.* London: Royal National Institute for the Deaf, 1976.

Speech and Speechreading:
Berger, K.W. *Speechreading: Principles and Methods.* Baltimore, Maryland: National Educational Press, 1972.
Jeffers, J., & Barley, M. *Speechreading (Lipreading).* Springfield, Illinois: Charles C. Thomas, 1971.
Ling, D. *Speech and the Hearing-impaired Child: Theory and Practice.* Washington, D.C.: Alexander Graham Bell Association for the Deaf, 1976.

Fingerspelling:
Carmel, S.J. *International Hand Alphabet Charts.* Rockville, Maryland: Author, 1975.

Signing and Sign Language:
Baker, C., & Battison, R. (Eds.). *Sign Language and the Deaf Community: Essays in Honor of William C. Stokoe.* Silver Spring, Maryland: National Association of the Deaf, 1980.

Baker, C., & Cokely, D. *American Sign Language: A Teachers Resource Text on Grammar and Culture.* Silver Spring, Maryland: T.J. Publishers, Inc., 1980.

Bergman, B. *Signed Swedish.* Stockholm: Swedish Board of Education, 1979.

Hoemann, H.H. *Communicating with Deaf People: A Resource Manual for Teachers and Students of American Sign Language.* Baltimore, Maryland: University Park Press, 1978.

Schlesinger, I.M. & Namir, L. (Eds.) *Sign Language of the Deaf: Psychological, Linguistic and Sociolinguistic Perspectives.* New York: Academic Press, 1978.

Siple, P. (Ed.). *Understanding Language Through Sign Language Research.* New York: Academic Press, 1978.

Stokoe, W.C. *Sign Language Structure: The First Linguistic Analysis of American Sign Language (Rev. ed.).* Silver Spring, Maryland: Linstok Press, 1978.

Woll, B., Kyle, J., & Deuchar, M. (Eds.). *Perspectives on British Sign Language and Deafness.* London: Croom Helm, 1981.

Language Acquisition:

Lenneberg, E.H. *Biological Foundations of Language.* New York: John Wiley and Sons, 1967.

Psychological Aspects:

Conrad, R. *The Deaf Schoolchild: Language and Cognitive Function.* London: Harper and Row, 1979.

Savage, R.D., Evans, L., & Savage, J.F. *Psychology and Communication in Deaf Children.* Sydney: Grune and Stratton, 1981. (Chapter 1 also provides a detailed account of the historical background to the use of oral and manual communication.)

1. Denton, D.M. Remarks in support of a system of total communication for deaf children. Communication Symposium, Maryland School for the Deaf, Frederick, 1970.

2. Merrill, E.C. President, Gallaudet College, Washington, D.C. Personal communication, 1973.

3. Stokoe, W.C. It takes two to total. Paper presented at Maryland School for the Deaf, Frederick, 1972.

4. Robson, P. Inspector of Special Education, Inner London Education Authority. Personal communication, June, 1980.

5. Montgomery, G.W.G., & Lines, A. Comparison of several single and combined methods of communicating with deaf children. Paper presented at Seminar on Visual Communication held at Northern Counties School for the Deaf, Newcastle upon Tyne, 1976.

6. Tervoort, B.T. What is the native language of a deaf child. Studies in honour of Professor B. Siertsema. University of Amsterdam, Institute for General Linguistics, 1979.

7. Isa, Y. Principal, Federation School for the Deaf, Penang, Malaysia. Personal communication, 1972.

8. Campbell, H. Jamaica Association for the Deaf, Kingston. Personal communication, 1980.

9. Campos, G. Mima Bravo Association, San Jose, Costa Rica. Personal communication, 1981.

10. Jeanes, R.C. Burwood State College, Victoria, Australia. Personal communication, March, 1981.

11. Jordan, I.K. Study of communication trends in education of the deaf in the United Kingdom, carried out from Research Unit, Donaldson's School, Edinburgh. In progress, April, 1981.

12. Evans, L. Study of total communication practices in schools, carried out from Gallaudet College, April, 1981.

13. McGuigan, F.J. Covert response patterns in processing language stimuli, final report. Hollins College, Virginia, 1972.

14. Washington State School for the Deaf. An introduction to manual English. Washington State School for the Deaf, Vancouver, 1972.

15. Young, Sr. L. St. Mary's School for the Deaf, Buffalo, New York. Personal communication, 1981.

Albright, M.A. Ear, eye or both. *Volta Review*, 1944, *46*, 11–13.

American Asylum for the Education and Instruction of Deaf and Dumb Persons. *Third Annual Report of the Directors*. Hartford, Connecticut: American Asylum, 1819.

Anderson, L.B. Sign language number systems and the numerical alphabet. In B. Frokjaer-Jensen (Ed.), *The Sciences of Deaf Signing*. Copenhagen: Audiologopedic Research Group, University of Copenhagen, 1980.

Anglin, L. *Word, Object and Concept Development*. New York: Norton, 1977.

Anthony, D. *Seeing Essential English*. Anaheim, California: Educational Services Division, Anaheim Union High School District, 1971.

Baker, C. How does Sim-Com fit into a bilingual approach to education? Paper presented at the Second National Symposium on Sign Language Research and Teaching, San Diego, 1978.

Baker, C., & Padden, C.A. Focusing on the nonmanual components of American Sign Language. In P. Siple (Ed.), *Understanding Language Through Sign Language Research*. New York: Academic Press, 1978.

Bates, E., Camaioni, L., & Volterra, V. The acquisition of performatives prior to speech. *Merrill-Palmer Quarterly*, 1975, *21*, 205–226.

Battison, R. Phonological deletion in American Sign Language. *Sign Language Studies*, 1974, *5*, 1–19.

Battison, R. *Lexical Borrowing in American Sign Language.* Silver Spring, Maryland: Linstok Press, 1978.

Bell, A.M. *English Visible Speech in Twelve Lessons.* Washington, D.C.: The Volta Bureau, 1895.

Bellugi, U. How signs express complex meaning. In C. Baker and R. Battison (Eds.), *Sign Language and the Deaf Community: Essays in Honor of William C. Stokoe.* Silver Spring, Maryland: National Association of the Deaf, 1980.

Bellugi, U., & Fischer, S. A comparison of sign language and spoken language: Rate and grammatical mechanisms. *Cognition*, 1972, *1*, 173–200.

Bellugi, U., Klima, E.S., & Siple, P. Remembering in signs. *Cognition*, 1975, *3*, 93–125.

Bellugi, U., & Siple, P. Remembering with and without words. In *Current Problems in Psycholinguistics.* Paris: Centre National de la Recherch Scientifique, 1974.

Bender, R.E. *The Conquest of Deafness* (Rev. ed.). Cleveland: Press of Case Western Reserve University, 1970.

Berger, K.W. *Speechreading: Principles and Methods.* Baltimore: National Educational Press, 1972.

Bergman, B. *Signed Swedish.* Stockholm: National Swedish Board of Education, 1979.

Bever, T. The cognitive basis for linguistic structures. In J.

Hayes (Ed.), *Cognition and the Development of Language.* New York: Wiley, 1970.

Binnie, C.A., Jackson, P.L., & Montgomery, A.A. Visual intelligibility of consonants: A lipreading screening test with implications for aural rehabilitation. *Journal of Speech and Hearing Disorders,* 1976, *41,* 530–539.

Blanton, R.L., & Brooks, P.H. Some psycholinguistic aspects of sign language. In I.M. Schlesinger and L. Namir (Eds.), *Sign Language of the Deaf: Psychological, Linguistic, and Sociolinguistic Perspectives.* New York: Academic Press, 1978.

Bonet, J.P. *Reduccion de las Letras, y Arte Para Ensenar a Hablar los Mudos.* Madrid: Par Francisco Abarca de Angelo (1620). English Translation by Dixon, H.N. *Simplification of the Letters of the Alphabet and Methods of Teaching Deaf-Mutes to Speak.* Harrogate: Farrar, 1890.

Bonvillian, J.D., & Nelson, K.E. Development of sign language in autistic children and other language-handicapped individuals. In P. Siple (Ed.), *Understanding Language Through Sign Language Research.* New York: Academic Press, 1978.

Bornstein, H. Signed English: A manual approach to English language development. *Journal of Speech and Hearing Disorders,* 1974, *39,* 330–343.

Bornstein, H. Systems of sign. In L.J. Bradford and W.G. Hardy (Eds.), *Hearing and Hearing Impairment.* New York: Grune and Stratton, 1979.

Bornstein, H., Hamilton, L.B., Saulnier, K.L., & Roy, H.L. *The Signed English Dictionary for Preschool and Ele-*

mentary Levels. Washington, D.C.: Gallaudet College Press, 1975.

Brain, W.R. Visual disorientation with special reference to lesions of the right cerebral hemisphere. *Brain*, 1941, *64*, 244–272.

Braybrook, D.M. Chapter 3 in P. Henderson (Ed.), *Methods of Communication Currently Used in the Education of Deaf Children.* London: Royal National Institute for the Deaf, 1976.

Brennan, M., Colville, M.D., & Lawson, L. *Words in Hand: A Structural Analysis of the Signs of British Sign Language.* British Sign Language Research Project, Moray House College, Edinburgh, 1980.

Brennan, M., & Hayhurst, A.B. The renaissance of British Sign Language. In C. Baker and R. Battison (Eds.), *Sign Language and the Deaf Community: Essays in Honor of William C. Stokoe.* Silver Spring, Maryland: National Association of the Deaf, 1980.

Brill, R.G. Chapter 14 in P. Henderson (Ed.), *Methods of Communication Currently Used in the Education of Deaf Children.* London: Royal National Institute for the Deaf, 1976.

Brill, R.G., & Fahey, J. A combination that works in a pre-school program for deaf children. *Hearing and Speech News*, 1971, *39*, 17–19.

Brown, R. *A First Language: The Early Stages.* Cambridge, Massachusetts: Harvard University Press, 1973.

Brown, R. Why are signed languages easier to learn than spoken languages? Paper presented at the First National

Symposium on Sign Language Research and Teaching, Chicago, 1977.

Bruhn, M. Methods of teaching lip reading: A symposium. Lip reading as living language. *Volta Review*, 1942, *44*, 636–638.

Bruhn, M. *The Mueller-Walle Method of Lipreading*. Washington, D.C.: The Volta Bureau, 1949.

Bruner, J.S. The course of cognitive growth. *American Psychologist*, 1964, *19*, 1–15.

Bulwer, J.B. *Chirologia: or, The Naturall Language of the Hand*. London: R. Whitaker, 1644.

Bulwer, J.B. *Philocophus: or, The Deafe and Dumbe Man's Friend*. London: Humphrey Moseley, 1648.

Burchett, J.H. *Lip Reading*. London: National Institute for the Deaf, 1950.

Butt, D., & Chreist, F.M. A speechreading test for young children. *Volta Review*, 1968, *70*, 225–235.

Child, D. *Psychology and the Teacher* (2nd ed.). London: Holt, Rinehart, and Winston, 1977.

Chomsky, N. *The Acquisition of Syntax in Children from 5-10*. Cambridge, Massachusetts: M.I.T. Press, 1969.

Clarke, B.R., & Ling, D. The effects of using cued speech: A follow-up study. *American Annals of the Deaf*, 1976, *121*, 23–34.

Clark, E. What's in a word? On the child's acquisition of semantics in his first language. In T. Moore (Ed.), *Cogni-*

tive Development and the Acquisition of Language. New York: Academic Press, 1973.

Clegg, D.G. *Pattern for the Listening Eye.* London: National Institute for the Deaf, 1953.

Clouser, R.A. The effect of vowel consonant ratio and sentence length on lipreading ability. *American Annals of the Deaf,* 1976, *121,* 513–518.

Cohen, E., Namir, L., & Schlesinger, I.M. *A New Dictionary of Sign Language.* The Hague: Mouton, 1977.

Cokely, D. *Pre-College Programs: Guidelines for Manual Communication.* Washington, D.C.: Gallaudet College, 1979.

Cokely, D. Sign language: Teaching, interpreting, and educational policy. In C. Baker and R. Battison (Eds.), *Sign Language and the Deaf Community: Essays in Honor of William C. Stokoe.* Silver Spring, Maryland: National Association of the Deaf, 1980.

Coltheart, M. Mysteries of reading in brain defects. *Rehabilitation, Great Britain,* 1980, *1,* 32–35.

Conrad, R. Short-term memory processes in the deaf. *British Journal of Psychology,* 1970, *61,* 179–195.

Conrad, R. The chronology of the development of covert speech in children. *Developmental Psychology,* 1971, *5,* 398–405.

Conrad, R. Chapter 21 in P. Henderson (Ed.), *Methods of Communication Currently Used in the Education of Deaf Children.* London: Royal National Institute for the Deaf, 1976.

Conrad, R. *The Deaf Schoolchild: Language and Cognitive Functioning.* London: Harper & Row, 1979.

Cornett, R.O. Cued Speech. *American Annals of the Deaf,* 1967, *112,* 3–13.

Craig, E. A supplement to the spoken word—the Paget-Gorman Sign System. In P. Henderson (Ed.), *Methods of Communication Currently Used in the Education of Deaf Children.* London: Royal National Institute for the Deaf, 1976.

Craig, W.N. Effects of preschool training on the development of reading and lipreading skills of deaf children. *American Annals of the Deaf,* 1964, *109,* 280–296.

Dalgarno, G. *Didascalocophus: or, The Deaf and Dumb Man's Tutor.* Oxford: Timothy Halton, 1680.

Davis, C. Chapter 11 in P. Henderson (Ed.), *Methods of Communication Currently Used in the Education of Deaf Children.* London: Royal National Institute for the Deaf, 1976.

Dawson, E.M. An experiment to investigate the optimal use of fingerspelling in a teacher/learning classroom situation. *Teacher of the Deaf,* 1976, *74,* 402–411.

De l'Epée, Abbé C.M. *Instruction des Sourds et Muets par la Voie des Signes Méthodiques.* Paris, 1776.

De l'Epée, Abbé C.M. *La Véritable Manière d'Instruire les Sourds et Muets, Confirmé par une Longue Expérience.* Paris: Chez Nyon L'Aîné, 1784.

Denes, P.B., & Pinson, E.N. *The Speech Chain.* Murray Hill, New Jersey: Bell Telephone Laboratories, 1963.

Denmark, J. Chapter 13 in P. Henderson (Ed.), *Methods of Communication Currently Used in the Education of Deaf Children*. London: Royal National Institute for the Deaf, 1976.

Department of Education and Science. *The Health of the School Child, 1962 and 1963*. London: Her Majesty's Stationery Office, 1964.

Department of Education and Science. *The Education of Deaf Children: The Possible Place of Fingerspelling and Signing*. London: Her Majesty's Stationery Office, 1968.

Dewey, G. *Relative Frequency of English Speech Sounds*. Cambridge, Massachusetts: Harvard University Press, 1923.

Di Carlo, L.M., & Kataja, R. An analysis of the Utley Lipreading Test. *Journal of Hearing Disorders*, 1951, *16*, 226–240.

Dodd, B. The role of vision in the perception of speech. *Perception*, 1977, *6*, 31–40.

Duffy, J.K. Audio-visual speech audiometry and a new audio and audio-visual speech perception index. *Maico Audiological Library Series*, 1967, *5*, 9.

Elstad, L.M. The deaf. In M.E. Frampton and E.D. Gall (Eds.), *Special Education for the Exceptional*. Boston: Porter Sargent, 1955.

Erber, N.P. Auditory and audiovisual reception of words in low-frequency noise by children with normal hearing and by children with impaired hearing. *Journal of Speech and Hearing Research*, 1971, *14*, 496–512.

Erber, N.P., & McMahan, D.A. Effects of sentence context on recognition of words through lipreading by deaf children. *Journal of Speech and Hearing Research*, 1976, *19*, 112–119.

Evans, L. Factors related to listening and lipreading. *Teacher of the Deaf*, 1960, *58*, 417–423.

Evans, L. Psychological factors related to lipreading. *Teacher of the Deaf*, 1965, *63*, 131–137.

Evans, L. Visual linguistic communication. Chapter 8 in P. Henderson (Ed.), *Methods of Communication Currently Used in the Education of Deaf Children*. London: Royal National Institute for the Deaf, 1976.

Evans, L. Visual communication in the deaf: Lipreading, fingerspelling and signing. Unpublished doctoral dissertation, University of Newcastle upon Tyne, 1978.

Evans, L. *Psycholinguistic Strategy for Deaf Children: The Integration of Oral and Manual Media*. Carlisle: The British Deaf Association, 1979.

Evans, L. Psycholinguistic perspectives on visual communication. Chapter 9 in B. Woll, J. Kyle, & M. Deuchar (Eds.), *Perspectives on British Sign Language and Deafness*. London: Croom Helm, 1981.

Ewing, A.W.G., & Ewing, E.C. *Teaching Deaf Children to Talk*. Manchester: The University Press, 1964.

Falberg, R.M. A pyscholinguistic view of the evolution, nature and value of the sign language of the deaf. Unpublished master's thesis, Wichita State University, 1964.

Farrar, A. *Historical Introduction to the English Translation of Bonet, 1620, Simplification of the Letters of the Alphabet and Method of Teaching Deaf Mutes to Speak.* Harrogate: Author, 1890.

Farrar, A. *Revision of Arnold: The Education of the Deaf.* London: National College of Teachers of the Deaf, 1923.

Farwell, R.M. Speech reading: A research review. *American Annals of the Deaf*, 1976, *121*, 19–30.

Fisher, C.G., & Husa, F.A. Fingerspelling intelligibility. *American Annals of the Deaf*, 1973, *118*, 508–510.

Fisher, M.T. *Improve Your Lipreading.* Washington, D.C.: The Volta Bureau, 1968.

Forchhammer, G. *On Nodvendigheden af Sikra Meddelelesmidler Dovstumme under Ervisingen.* Copenhagen: J. Frimodts, Fortag, 1903. Text of English translation, *The Need of a Sure Means of Communication in the Instruction of the Deaf*, Royal National Institute for the Deaf Library, London.

Freeman, R.D. Some psychiatric reflections on the controversy over methods of communication in the life of the deaf. In P. Henderson (Ed.), *Methods of Communication Currently Used in the Education of Deaf Children.* London: Royal National Institute for the Deaf, 1976.

Freeman, R.D. Medical evaluation: An overview. *Directions*, 1980, *1*(4), 46–47.

Freeman, R.D., Carbin, C.F., & Boese, R.J. *Can't Your Child Hear? A Guide for Those Who Care about Deaf Children.* Baltimore: University Park Press, 1981.

Friedman, L.A. Space, time, and person reference in American Sign Language. *Language*, 1975, *51*, 940–961.

Frishberg, N. Arbitrariness and iconicity: Historical change in American Sign Language. *Language*, 1975, *51*, 696–719.

Frishberg, N. A linguist looks at sign language teaching. Paper presented at First National Symposium on Sign Language Research and Teaching, Chicago, 1977.

Fry, D.B. The reception of speech. In E. Whetnall & D.B. Fry, *The Deaf Child*. Springfield, Illinois: Charles C. Thomas, 1964.

Garretson, M.D. Committee report defining total communication. *Proceedings of the Forty-Eighth Meeting of the Conference of Executives of American Schools for the Deaf*, Rochester, New York, 1976a.

Garretson, M.D. Total communication. In R. Frisina (Ed.), A Bicentennial Monograph on Hearing Impairment: Trends in the U.S.A. *Volta Review*, 1976b, 78(4).

Givens, D. Infantile reflexive behaviours and nonverbal communication. *Sign Language Studies*, 1977, *16*, 219–236.

Gleason, H. *Descriptive Linguistics*. New York: Holt, Rinehart and Winston, 1961.

Goldin-Meadow, S., & Feldman, H. The creation of a communication system: A study of deaf children of hearing parents. *Sign Language Studies*, 1975, *8*, 225–236.

Goldstein, M.A. *Problems of the Deaf*. St. Louis, Missouri: The Laryngoscope Press, 1933.

Gordon, J.C. *Notes and Observations upon the Education of the Deaf.* Washington, D.C.: The Volta Bureau, 1892.

Grove, C., O'Sullivan, F.D., & Rodda, M. Communication and language in severely deaf adolescents. *British Journal of Psychology*, 1979, *70*, 531–540.

Gustason, G., Pfetzing, D., & Zawolkow, E. *Signing Exact English.* Rossmoor, California: Modern Signs Press, 1972.

Gustason, G., & Woodward, J. (Eds.). *Recent Developments in Manual English—Papers Presented at a Special Institute.* Washington, D.C.: Gallaudet College, 1973.

Hansen, B. *Aspects of Deafness and Total Communication in Denmark.* Copenhagen: The Center for Total Communication, 1980.

Hanson, V.L. When a word is not the sum of its letters: Fingerspelling and spelling. Paper presented at the National Symposium on Sign Language Research and Teaching, Boston, 1980.

Hardy, M. Speechreading. In H. Davis & S.R. Silverman (Eds.), *Hearing and Deafness.* New York: Holt, Rinehart and Winston, 1970.

Haugen, E. Linguistics and language planning. *Sociolinguistics: Proceedings of the 1964 UCLA Sociolinguistics Conference.* The Hague: Mouton, 1966.

Hebb, D.O. Intelligence in man after large removals of cerebral tissue: Defects following right temporal lobotomy. *Journal of General Psychology*, 1939, *21*, 437–446.

Herriot, P. *An Introduction to the Psychology of Language.* London: Methuen, 1970.

Hester, M.S. Manual communication. *Report of the Proceedings of the Forty-First Meeting of the Convention of American Instructors of the Deaf.* Washington, D.C.: U.S. Government Printing Office, 1964, 211–221.

Hicks, W.M., & Hicks, D.E. The Usher's Syndrome adolescent—Programming implications for school administrators, teachers, and residential advisors. *American Annals of the Deaf,* 1981, *126,* 422–431.

Hoemann, M.W. Categorical coding of Sign and English in short-term memory by deaf and hearing subjects. In P. Siple (Ed.), *Understanding Language Through Sign Language Research.* New York: Academic Press, 1978.

Holcomb, R.K. Three years of the total approach—1968–71. *Report of the Proceedings of the Forty-Fifth Meeting of the Convention of American Instructors of the Deaf.* Washington, D.C.: U.S. Government Printing Office, 1972, 165–183.

Hopkins, L.A. The relationship between degrees of deafness and response to acoustic training. *Volta Review,* 1953, *55,* 23.

Hudgins, C.V. The development of communication skills among profoundly deaf children in an auditory training programme. In A.W.G. Ewing (Ed.), *The Modern Educational Treatment of Deafness.* Manchester: The University Press, 1960.

Hutton, C. Combining auditory and visual stimuli in aural rehabilitation. *Volta Review,* 1959, *61,* 316–319.

Ingram, D. *Phonological Disability in Children.* New York: Elsevier, 1976.

Jakobson, R. [*Child Language, Aphasia and Phonological Universals*] (A. Keiler, translator). The Hague: Mouton, 1968. (Originally published 1941).

Jeffers, J., & Barley, M. *Speechreading (Lipreading)*. Springfield, Illinois: Charles C. Thomas, 1971.

Jensema, C.J., Karchmer, M.A., & Trybus, R.J. *The Rated Speech Intelligibility of Hearing Impaired Children: Basic Relationships and a Detailed Analysis*. Office of Demographic Studies, Series R, Number 6. Washington, D.C.: Gallaudet College, 1978.

Jordan, I.K., Gustason, G., & Rosen, R. Current communication trends at programs for the deaf. *American Annals of the Deaf*, 1976, *121*(6), 527–532.

Jordan, I.K., Gustason, G., & Rosen, R. An update on communication trends at programs for the deaf. *American Annals of the Deaf*, 1979, *124*, 350–357.

Kaplan, E., & Kaplan, G. The prelinguistic child. In J. Eliot (Ed.), *Human Development and Cognitive Processes*. New York: Holt, Rinehart and Winston, 1971.

Kimura, D. Speech lateralization in young children as determined by an auditory test. *Journal of Comparative and Physiological Psychology*, 1963, *56*, 899–902.

Klima, E.S., & Bellugi, U. *The Signs of Language*. Cambridge, Massachusetts: Harvard University Press, 1979.

Klopping, H. Language understanding of deaf students under three auditory-visual stimulus conditions. *American Annals of the Deaf*, 1972, *117*(3), 389–396.

Knight, D.L. A general model of English language development in hearing-impaired children. *Directions*, 1979, 1(1), 9–28.

Kuczaj, S. On the acquisition of a semantic system. *Journal of Verbal Learning and Verbal Behaviour*, 1975, 14(4), 340–358.

Lane, H., Boyes-Braem, P., & Bellugi, U. Preliminaries to a distinctive feature analysis of handshapes in American Sign Language. *Cognitive Psychology*, 1976, 8, 263–289.

Lenneberg, E.H. *Biological Foundations of Language*. New York: John Wiley and Sons, 1967.

Levitt, D., & Groode, J. Methods of teaching fingerspelling. Paper presented at the National Symposium on Sign Language Research and Teaching, Boston, 1980.

Levitt, H. Language communication skills of deaf children, 1973/75. Proceedings of Language Assessment for the Hearing Impaired—a Work Study Institute, New York State Education Department, 1976.

Levy, J. Psychological implications of bilateral asymmetry. In S.J. Dimond and J.G. Beaumont (Eds.), *Hemisphere Function in the Brain*. New York: John Wiley and Sons, 1974.

Lewis, D.N. Lipreading skills of hearing impaired children in regular schools. *Volta Review*, 1972, 74, 303–311.

Ling, D. *Speech and the Hearing-impaired Child: Theory and Practice*. Washington, D.C.: Alexander Graham Bell Association for the Deaf, 1976.

Ling, D., & Clarke, B.R. Cued Speech: An evaluative study. *American Annals of the Deaf*, 1975, *120*, 480–488.

Lowell, E.L. Research in speechreading: Some relationships to language development and implications for the class-room teacher. *Report of the Proceedings of the Thirty-Ninth Meeting of the Convention of American Instructors of the Deaf*. Washington, D.C.: U.S. Government Printing Office, 1960, 68–73.

Lowell, E.L. Chapter 5 in P. Henderson (Ed.), *Methods of Communication Currently Used in the Education of Deaf Children*. London: Royal National Institute for the Deaf, 1976.

MacNamara, J. Cognitive basis of language learning in infants. *Psychological Review*, 1972, *79*, 1–13.

Markides, A. The speech of deaf and partially-hearing children with special reference to factors affecting intelligibility. *British Journal of Disorders of Communication*, 1970, *5*, 126–140.

Markides, A. Rehabilitation of people with acquired deafness in adulthood. *British Journal of Audiology*, Supplement 1, 1977.

Marmor, G., Strauss, G., & Petitto, L. Simultaneous communication in the classroom: How well is English grammar represented? *Sign Language Studies*, 1979, *23*, 99–136.

Mayberry, R.I. Manual communication. In H. Davis and S.R. Silverman (Eds.), *Hearing and Deafness* (4th ed.). New York: Holt, Rinehart and Winston, 1978.

McFie, J. Factors of the brain. *Bulletin of British Psychological Society*, 1972, *25*, 11–14.

McKeever, W.F., Hoemann, H.W., Florian, V.A., & Van Deventer, A.D. Evidence of minimal cerebral asymmetries for the processing of English words and American Sign Language in the congenitally deaf. *Neuropsychologia*, 1976, *14*, 413–423.

McNally, J. *The First Ladybird Key Words Picture Dictionary*. Loughborough: Wills and Hepworth, 1965.

Mead, M. Vicissitudes of the study of the total communication process. In T.A. Sebeck (Ed.), *Approaches to Semiotics*. The Hague: Mouton.

Meadow, K.P. Early manual communication in relation to the deaf child's intellectual, social, and communicative functioning. *American Annals of the Deaf*, 1968, *113*, 29–41.

Meadow, K.P. A developmental perspective on the use of manual communication with deaf children. In P. Henderson (Ed.), *Methods of Communication Currently Used in the Education of Deaf Children*. London: Royal National Institute for the Deaf, 1976.

Milan International Congress on Education of the Deaf. *Report of the Proceedings*. London: W.H. Allen & Company, 1880.

Montgomery, G.W.G. The relationship of oral skills to manual communication in profoundly deaf adolescents. *American Annals of the Deaf*, 1966, *111*, 557–565.

Montgomery G.W.G. A factorial study of communication

and ability in deaf school leavers. *British Journal of Educational Psychology*, 1968, *38*(3), 27–37.

Montgomery, G.W.G. The integration of the oral-manual language ability of profoundly deaf children. In P. Henderson (Ed.), *Methods of Communication Currently Used in the Education of Deaf Children*. London: Royal National Institute for the Deaf, 1976.

Moores, D.F. Neo-oralism and the education of the deaf in the Soviet Union. *Exceptional Children*, 1972, *38*, 377–384.

Morkovin, B.V. Experiment in teaching deaf preschool children in the Soviet Union. *Volta Review*, 1960, *62*, 260–268.

Moser, H.M., O'Neill, J.J., Oyer, H.J., Wolfe, S.M., Abernathy, E.A., & Schowe, B.M. *Hand Signals: Fingerspelling*. Technical Report, Ohio State University Research Foundation, 1958.

Myklebust, H.R. *The Psychology of Deafness*. New York: Grune and Stratton, 1964.

Namir, L., & Schlesinger, I.M. The grammar of sign language. In I.M. Schlesinger and L. Namir (Eds.), *Sign Language of the Deaf: Psychological, Linguistic, and Sociolinguistic Perspectives*. New York: Academic Press, 1978.

Neville, H.J. The functional significance of cerebral specialization. In R.W. Rieber (Ed.), *The Neuropsychology of Language: Essays in Honor of Eric Lenneberg*. New York: Plenum Press, 1976.

Neyhus, A.I. *Speechreading Failure in Deaf Children*. Washington, D.C.: Office of Education, Department of Health, Education and Welfare, 1969.

Nicholls, G.H. Cued Speech and the reception of spoken language. Unpublished master's thesis, McGill University, 1979.

Nix, G.W. Total communication: A review of the studies offered in its support. *Volta Review*, 1975, 77, 470–494.

Numbers, M.E., & Hudgins, C.V. Speech perception in present day education for deaf children. *Volta Review*, 1948, 50, 449–456.

O'Neill, J.J. An exploratory investigation of lipreading ability amongst normal hearing students. *Speech Monograph*, 1951, 18, 309–311.

O'Neill, J.J. Contributions of the visual components of oral symbols to speech comprehension. *Journal of Speech and Hearing Disorders*, 1954, 19, 429–439.

O'Neill, J.J., and Davidson, J.L. Relationship between lipreading ability and five psychological factors. *Journal of Speech and Hearing Disorders*, 1956, 21, 478–481.

O'Rourke, T.J. *A Basic Course in Manual Communication*. Silver Spring, Maryland: National Association of the Deaf, 1973.

Paterson, A., & Zangwill, O.L. Disorders of visual space perception associated with lesions of the right cerebral hemisphere. *Brain*, 1944, 67, 331–358.

Pauls, M.D. Speechreading. In H. Davis and S.R. Silverman (Eds.), *Hearing and Deafness*. New York: Holt, Rinehart and Winston, 1960.

Piaget, J. *Play, Dreams, and Imitation in Childhood*. New York: Norton, 1962.

Pintner, R. Speech reading tests for the deaf. *Journal of Applied Psychology*, 1929, *13*, 220–225.

Pollard, G., & Neumaier, R. Vision characteristics of deaf students. *American Annals of the Deaf*, 1974, *119*, 740–745.

Prall, J. Lipreading and hearing aids combine for better comprehension. *Volta Review*, 1957, *59*, 64–65.

Prinz, P.M., & Prinz, E.A. Simultaneous acquisition of ASL and spoken English (In a hearing child of a deaf mother and hearing father). *Sign Language Studies*, 1979, *25*, 283–296.

Quigley, S. *The Influence of Fingerspelling on the Development of Language, Communication, and Educational Achievement in Deaf Children*. Urbana, Illinois: University of Illinois, 1969.

Rawlings, B.W. *Characteristics of Hearing Impaired Students by Hearing Status: 1970-71*. Office of Demographic Studies, Series D, Number 10. Washington, D.C.: Gallaudet College, 1973.

Rawlings, B.W., Trybus, R.J., & Biser, J. (Eds.). *A Guide to College/Career Programs for Deaf Students*. Washington, D.C.: Gallaudet College, 1981.

Reed, M. Communication in deaf children. In P. Henderson (Ed.), *Methods of Communication Currently Used in the Education of Deaf Children*. London: Royal National Institute for the Deaf, 1976.

Reeves, J.K. The use of hearing aids by children with defective hearing. *Teacher of the Deaf*, 1961, *59*, 181–190.

Reeves, J.K. The whole personality approach to oralism in the education of the deaf. In P. Henderson (Ed.), *Methods of Communication Currently Used in the Education of Deaf Children*. London: Royal National Institute for the Deaf, 1976.

Reich, P.A., & Bick, M. An empirical investigation of some claims made in support of visible English. *American Annals of the Deaf*, 1976, *121*, 573–577.

Reich, P.A., Nickerson, N., Bick, M., Mierle, S., & Michal, D. Variables Affecting the Comprehension of Visible English. University of Toronto, Department of Linguistics, 1976.

Reid, G. A preliminary investigation in the testing of lip-reading achievement. *Journal of Speech and Hearing Disorders*, 1947, *12*, 77–82.

Reimer, B.L. A viable classroom model for using various communication modes. *American Annals of the Deaf*, 1979, *124*, 838–846.

Riekehof, L.L. *The Joy of Signing*. Springfield, Missouri: Gospel Publishing House, 1978.

Rodda, M., Godsave, B., & Stevens, J. Some aspects of the

development of young hearing-impaired children. *American Annals of the Deaf*, 1974, *119*, 729–735.

Rosch, E. On the internal structure of perceptual and semantic categories. In T. Moore (Ed.), *Cognitive Development and the Acquisition of Language*. New York: Academic Press, 1973.

Ross, M., Kessler, M.E., Philips, M.E., & Lerman, J.W. Visual, auditory, and combined mode presentations of the WIPI test to hearing-impaired children. *Volta Review*, 1972, *74*, 90–92.

Savage, R.D., Evans, L., & Savage, J.F. *Psychology and Communication in Deaf Children*. Sydney: Grune and Stratton, 1981.

Schlesinger, H.S., & Meadow, K. *Sound and Sign: Childhood Deafness and Mental Health*. Berkeley, California: University of California Press, 1972.

Scouten, E. Total communication in a new perspective. *Florida School Herald*, 1973, 72, 1–2.

Shannon, C.E. A mathematical theory of communication. *Bell System Technical Journal*, 1948, *27*, 379–423; 623–656.

Sicard, R.A.C. *Théorie des Signes*. Paris: De L'Imprimerie d'a clo, Treuttel et Wurtz, 1818.

Simmons, A.A. Factors related to lipreading. *Journal of Speech and Hearing Research*, 1959, *2*, 340–352.

Siple, P. Linguistic and psychological properties of American Sign Language: An overview. In P. Siple (Ed.), *Under-*

standing Language Through Sign Language Research.
New York: Academic Press, 1978.

Siple, P., Fischer, S., & Bellugi, U. Memory for nonseman-
tic attributes of American Sign Language signs and English words. *Journal of Verbal Learning and Verbal Behaviour,* 1977, *16,* 561–574.

Skarakis, E.A., & Prutting, C.A. Early communication: Semantic functions and communicative intentions in the
communication of the preschool child with impaired
hearing. *American Annals of the Deaf,* 1977, *122,* 382–
391.

Smith, F. *Understanding Reading: A Psycholinguistic
Analysis of Reading and Learning to Read.* (2nd ed.).
New York: Holt, Rinehart and Winston, 1978.

Stevenson, E.A. *A Study of the Educational Achievement
of Deaf Children of Deaf Parents.* Berkeley, California:
California School for the Deaf.

Stokoe, W.C. *Sign Language Structure: An Outline of the
Visual Communication Systems of the American Deaf.*
Studies in Linguistics: Occasional Paper No., 8. Buffalo,
New York: University of Buffalo, 1960.

Stokoe, W.C. *Sign Language Structure: The First Linguistic
Analysis of American Sign Language,* (rev. ed.). Silver
Spring, Maryland: Linstok Press, 1978.

Stokoe, W.C., Casterline, D.C., & Croneberg, C.G. *A Dictionary of American Sign Language on Linguistic Principles.* Washington, D.C.: Gallaudet College Press, 1965.

Stuckless, E.R. An interpretive review of research on manual communication in the education of deaf children: Language development and information transmission. In P. Henderson (Ed.), *Methods of Communication Currently Used in the Education of Deaf Children*. London: Royal National Institute for the Deaf, 1976.

Stuckless, E.R., & Birch, J.W. The influence of early manual communication on the linguistic development of deaf children. *American Annals of the Deaf*, 1966, *111*, 452–460.

Taaffe, G., & Wong, W. *Studies of Variables in Lipreading Stimulus Materials*. Los Angeles: John Tracy Clinic Research Paper III, 1957.

Trybus, R. J., & Karchmer, M. A. School achievement scores of hearing impaired children: National data on achievement status and growth patterns. *American Annals of the Deaf*, 1977, *122*, 62–69.

Valade, Y-L.R. *Édutes sur la Lexicologie et la Grammaire du Langage Naturel des Signes*. Paris, 1854.

Van Uden, A. *Proceedings of the Annual Conference of Heads of Schools for the Deaf and Partially Hearing*. Manchester: Department of Audiology and Education of the Deaf, Manchester University, 1974.

Verney, A. Planning for a preferred future. In P. Henderson (Ed.), *Methods of Communication Currently Used in the Education of Deaf Children*. London: Royal National Institute for the Deaf, 1976.

Vernon, M. Mind over mouth: A rationale for total communication. *Volta Review*, 1972, *74*, 529–540.

(Eds.), *Proceedings of the Tenth Regional Meeting of the Chicago Linguistic Society*, Chicago, Illinois.

Wolff, J.G. Language before speech: A new phonetically-based combined system for the development of language in deaf children. *Teacher of the Deaf*, 1971, *69*, 96–114.

Wood, K.S., & Blakely, R.W. The association of lipreading and the ability to understand distorted speech. *Western Speech*, 1953, *17*, 259–261.

Woodward, J. Some characteristics of Pidgin Sign English. *Sign Language Studies*, 1973, *3*, 39–46.

Woodward, J. Historical bases of American Sign Language. In P. Siple (Ed.), *Understanding Language Through Sign Language Research*. New York: Academic Press, 1978.

Woodward, M.F., & Barber, C.G. Phoneme perception in lipreading. *Journal of Speech and Hearing Research*, 1960, *3*, 213–222.

Woodward, M.F., & Lowell, E.E. *A Linguistic Approach to the Education of Aurally-Handicapped Children*. United States Department of Health, Education and Welfare Project 907, 1964.

Young, D. *Group Reading Test*. London: University of London Press, 1968.

NAME INDEX

This book was typeset in 10/13 Trump Medieval by Mid-Atlantic Photo Composition of Baltimore, Maryland. It was printed on 60 lb. Warren's Olde Style by Fairfield Graphics (Arcata Book Group) of Fairfield, Pennsylvania. The text was designed by Donna Simons.